Blues & Rock Harp Positions Made Easy

By David Harp

© 1997 Musical I. Press, Inc.
P.O. Box 1561
Montpelier, Vermont 05602

ISBN 0 - 918321- 83 - 2

Book design and Cover Photo

by *Rita Ricketson*

Distributed to the music trade
by Music Sales Corporation

Distributed to the book trade
by Publishers Group West

Printed in the State of Vermont
in the United States of America by
L. Brown & Sons Printing, Inc.

Table of Contents

PART ONE

*NOTE: Each additional position, Third through Twelfth,
also features some or all of the sections listed above.
But to save space in this Table of Contents, I will only
list the "unusual features" of each position below.*

Dedication

I would like to dedicate this book to those unknown musical geniuses who decided not to play Major and Minor Scale songs on our favoite instrument.

No one knows their names. But they added momentum to the most important musical event of our century and the last, if they did not help to invent it outright. I'm speaking, of course, of the birth of the Blues — America's greatest contribution to the culture of the planet.

And to Lily — Already an "original" at Two!

— David Harp

A Few Other Books by David Harp

Instant Blues Harmonica (Volumes I and II)

Instant Chromatic Harmonica: The Blues/Jazz Improvisation Method

Instant Guitar

Instant Flute

The Instant Harmonica Kit for Kids

Harmonica Positions

The Three Minute Meditator

Me and My Harmonica

Instant Blues/Rock Harmonica: The Video

Make Me Musical: Instant Harmonica, A Complete Musical Education for Kids

Metaphysical Fitness: A Complete 30 Day Plan for Your Mental, Emotional, and Spiritual Health (with Dr. Nina Feldman)

The Three Minute Meditator Audiotape (with Dr. Nina Feldman)

How To Whistle Like A Pro (with Jason Serinus)

Bending the Blues

EarthCards (with The Write for Action Group)

The New Three Minute Meditator

The Instant Rhythm Kit

In Hot Water: How To Save Your Back, Neck, and Shoulders In Ten Minutes A Day (With Dr. P. Horay)

How To Play Country & Western Harmonica

Music Theory Made Easy

Instant Harmonica for Kids (Video)

The Pocket Harmonica Songbook

Three Minutes to™ Blues Harmonica (Video)

Blues & Rock Harmonica Made Easy

and more on the way!

PART ONE

I've designed this book to be used by many levels of players, from near-beginners to near pro-level players. Whether you're just starting to think about bending, or whether you've got a band and can overblow and over-draw better than most — I've got some tasty stuff for you!

By the way: if you're a *total* beginner, you should probably start out with one of my more general beginner's methods that are described on page 93 (Why don't you read that page right now?). *Then* come back to this page.

But if you can already play even the simplest Blues lick, or a single folk song — keep reading, and soon you'll be ready to play — with positions!

Part One covers what positions are, and why they work. I'll explain concepts like "key," and "scale," and teach you how to use the four most important scales to compose songs or improvise "riffs" and "solos." I'll describe the "Position Myths," and how they developed.

But Part One will not require much technical ability on your part — even near-beginners will be able to demonstrate all the examples for themselves. For instance, I'll barely mention the important technique of "bending" notes, although some of the "Blues Scale" examples I give you use a few bent notes. Whenever I give you an example with bent notes, I will also include a simplified "non-bent" version of that example.

Plus, I've used a "star system" to tell you how hard each song, scale, and riff is. You'll also be able to play *any* of the "one star" ★ songs and riffs right away — in any position! (I love that wild "Sixth Position," and it's super easy, too!) But ★★ riffs use bends, and ★★★★ = **HARD!**

Part Two starts out with an explanation of the "Twelve Bar Blues," and contains all of the actual "how tos" on positions. Twelve Bars, riffs, scales, solos — material for *every level* of player is in here, and for every position!

Part Three contains The PositionFinder™ Method. You'll never worry about which harp to use when, again!

Using The Box System

Positions are incredibly tied in to every part of good harp playing. This means that you need to learn at least a little bit of music theory, some harmonica history, an easy notation system, and a few other things before I can even give you a good definition of positions!

I'll try to keep it as short, and easy, as possible. But I know that some of you (especially more advanced players) may be in a hurry to get to the riffs and scales of Part Two, or to The PositionFinder™ Method in Part Three.

> So I've put really crucial Part One information into two kinds of boxes. The more the box stands out, the more important the information!

If you're really in a rush, you can: Skim through the pages. Read *every* **section title,** and then read that whole section if it seems like it would be interesting or important to you. For example, if you're an "intermediate" player, you'd want to read the entire next section.

Otherwise, you can just read each box. You'll understand the most important concepts, and also get to Part Two in no time! Then come back and read the rest of each section, while your lips are cooling off!

RutBusters™

Maybe you are already using the two most popular positions (which are "First" and "Second" Positions, otherwise known as "cross harp" and "straight harp"). But even if you are, you may well be a victim of some very common myths about positions (I used to be, too!).

These myths limit us, and keep us stuck in narrow "ruts," playing the same old stuff over and over. If this is your problem — I guarantee you that before the end of this book, you'll be breaking out of your ruts in ways that you never imagined! In fact, some harp players call my positions package "The RutBuster™"!

> Advanced Players: Use the boxes (at least) in Part One to make sure you know how to create riffs and solos from scales. You'll get to the hard stuff soon!

A Note for "Ear" Players

Some people just seem to have a hard time learning music, by reading about it. That's why I always have audiotapes as well as books! They're on page 93.

Which Harmonica to Use?

> You can use any "standard-tuned" or "diatonic" or "Major-tuned" (also called a "Blues harmonica" or "Marine Band type") ten hole harmonica with this book.

In most of my diagrams, I use a ten hole harmonica in the "key of C" as an example, since C is the most widely owned harmonica key.

But if you plan to use this book along with the audiotape, you will need a harmonica in the key of "A." Why? Because the key of A harmonica is the easiest to get all of the necessary "bends" and "blow bends" on.

Of course, if you plan to play with other musicians, eventually you'll want to get lots of different key harps. I recommend starting out with ten hole harmonicas in the keys of C, A, and F — but more on that, later.

If you don't know about keys, or bending, yet — just keep on reading. You'll find out!

What *Are* "Positions?"

I'll be giving you different definitions of the term "Positions" throughout this book. The more you know about them, the better a definition I can offer. This one's pretty general — we could call it **"Definition Zero!"**

As I said on the back cover, harmonica "positions" are nothing more than a very specific and simplified form of **music theory** developed especially for the harmonica. This form of harmonica music theory is based on playing different **"scales,"** although the players who invented positions may not have known this consciously.

Why Are Positions?

Harmonica positions were invented to deal with the following two facts.

• The harmonica was created by people who had been trained in the **European** musical tradition. They wanted an instrument that could play Beethoven, or Bach, or German folk melodies, easily. More easily, in fact, than any other instrument.

• Later on, people who had been brought up in the **African-American** musical tradition wanted to use the harmonica (by now becoming known as a "Blues harp") to play Blues and then rock style music.

European music uses certain **"scales,"** or groups of notes. African-American music uses different scales. That's why the different positions came about — they were originally used to play these different scales in the easiest ways possible.

Why "Positions" are Weird

There are two main reasons that harmonica positions are often considered hard to understand, or even flaky and strange, by both harp players and by other musicians.

• Firstly, this form of harmonica music theory (positions) was developed by musicians who were **not formally trained** in music, and had probably never studied any regular (non-harmonica) music theory.

• Secondly, the ten hole (also called the "diatonic") harmonica is an unusual instrument. Unlike pianos, guitars, flutes, violins, or chromatic harmonicas, certain notes on the ten hole harmonica are left out, certain notes are repeated, and many notes are available only by the odd technique of "bending" notes.

Since positions were developed by great harp players who were not great music theorists, using an instrument that was tuned strangely from the very beginning — positions are quirky, and incomplete, and at least a bit contradictory.

This is one reason why positions always seem hard for beginners to understand. And a little strange to any harp player who doesn't already know music theory (which most of us, myself formerly included, don't).

Positions and Playing Along with Others

Positions are even more strange to anyone who *does* know music theory, but doesn't play harp. Guitar players and people in bands (especially those who know some music theory) often look at us harp players as though we're kind of ignorant, and a little dangerous, too. They are never quite sure which key harmonica we should be using to play which song. And, even worse, they're not at all sure that we know, either!

> A harp player who understands the different positions and can use them with confidence (like you will, soon) is a great relief to other musicians.

Good News and Bad: The "Positions Myth"

The good news is that lots of Blues and rock harp players already know about positions. The bad news is that much of what they know, may be wrong!

When I started playing, I though positions had to do with how you held your hands when you played. Then I "learned" that folk songs were always played in "Straight Position," and that Blues were always played in "Cross Position." And that's as far as I got, for many years.

I would occasionally hear a player, live or recorded, playing amazing harmonica Blues in ways that I just couldn't duplicate. Charlie Musselwhite, Magic Dick, Little Walter, Will Scarlett — they were using a ten hole harmonica, but getting sounds and note combinations that didn't seem to be in *my* harp!

Eventually I began to study music theory, and I learned what positions really are. I started to use them to play in the styles of my heroes — slow, sad, organ-like Musselwhite Blues; and fast, screaming, Magic Dick high end riffs. Learning to use positions more fully has added a lot to my playing. And I'd like to help you add to yours!

> Many of us experienced harp players already "use" one or two positions. But if we don't understand why we do what we do, we limit ourselves. The more we know about positions, the better we can play!

I won't be able to give you a really complete explanation of what the positions are until we've talked about "key," and "scales," and a few other things. But I will tell you what positions can do for us.

What Positions Do for Us

There are two really important reasons for Blues and rock harp players to understand positions.

- Positions tell use **which "key" harmonica** to use to play along with **what "key" music.**

- And positions help us to play the different **"scales"** that all good musicians use to create and play music.

> So positions tell us which **"key"** harmonica to use when. They can also help us choose which notes — in the form of **"scales"** — to use on that harmonica.

What "Key" is Your Harp?

Positions tell us what is the best possible **"key"** harmonica to play along with what "key" music. I'll be able to give you a more complete definition of "key" later. But for now, the I will use the term "key of a harmonica" to mean the little *note letter names* printed on the harmonica.

Standard ten hole harmonicas come in twelve different keys. The note letter names for these twelve keys are:

G	**Ab**	**A**	**Bb**	**B**	**C**	
	Db	**D**	**Eb**	**E**	**F**	**Gb**

These letter names tell you the lowest note of that harmonica (the 1 hole out). If the 1 out note is a "C" note, we call it a **"C harmonica."** If the 1 out note is a **"Db"** **(D flat)** note, we call it a **"Db harmonica,"** and so on.

A harmonica whose 1 out note is an E is often called a **"key of E harmonica."** In music theory terms, it's really more accurate to say "E harmonica" rather than "key of E harmonica." But expressions like "key of G harmonica" or "key of F harp" are often used, so we'll let them alone!

Letter Names for Notes (# and b)

Note letter names come from the keys of the piano. Each white key has a name from A to G, and each black key has *two names*. "Flat" or "b" means "lower than." "Sharp" or "#" means "higher than."

So the black key between the keys C and D can be called either **C#** (meaning higher than C) or **Db** (meaning lower than D).

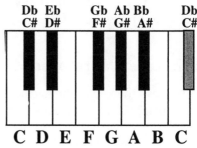

Most harmonica manufacturers use flat names (the "b" symbols) rather than sharp names (the "#" symbols) on the instrument. So you are more likely to have an Eb harp than a D# harp. But not all of them use flat names.

And do you want to play with other musicians, and use lots of different key harmonicas? Then you will need to know both names for each black note, and that an A# harp is the same as a Bb harp, and so on. Here's a little chart to help you remember.

A# = Bb	**C# = Db**	**D# = Eb**	**F# = Gb**	**G# = Ab**

Counting Half Steps

It is also a very good idea to memorize the twelve notes (and their names) that exist on the keyboard.

A#		C#		D#		F#		G#	
A	Bb	B	C	Db	D	Eb	E	F	Gb	G	Ab

Each of these above notes is said to be **"one half step"** apart — that is, each note on the piano keyboard is "one half step" above the next lowest note. So, for example, the note "C" is said to be "three half steps" above the note "A." Knowing how to "count" half steps can be very helpful when you are figuring out which key harmonica to use with which key music!

> If you don't really understand the little note letters, like C or Bb — printed on your harmonica, read this whole section. Knowing them will come in handy when you play with other musicians.

Flat Letter Names for the Blues

Though not 100% correct from the viewpoint of classical music theory, in Blues music it's more common to use flat names (b symbols) than sharp (#) names. So since we're mainly concerned with Blues (and its offspring, rock) I'll mostly use flat names for notes from here on. It's easier than writing out stuff like "A# or Bb" every single time!

What "Key" is the Music In?

Any piece of music — Blues, rock, or Beethoven — is also said to be in a particular "key," using the note letter names (after we've studied scales, we'll see why this is). So musicians get used to hearing things like these:

"Ready for a Blues in the key of C?"

"Here's some fast rock in G." Or...

"Let's play the fourth movement of Beethoven's Ninth right now, in the key of F."

What Key Harmonica Do I Use?

How does the key of the harmonica fit in with the key of the music? That's what this whole book is about.

You see, if we always used a key of C harmonica to play music that is "in the key of C," and if we always used a key of F harmonica to play music that is "in the key of F" — life would be easy, and positions would be unneccessary. But it's more complicated than that.

> Harmonicas come in twelve different **"keys."** These are indicated by *note letter names*, from A to G, printed right on the harmonica.
>
> Music also comes in different keys, also indicated by note letter names from A to G. I'll talk more about this, soon.

Positions tell us which key harmonica to use with which key music.

It's a bit complicated, since good players can use any single key harmonica (for example, a "C" harp) to play along with five different keys of music! Your "C" harp can play great Blues or rock music in the keys of C, G, D, A, or E — If you understand positions! And really advanced players can use *any* single key of harp to play along with **twelve** different keys of music.

Or, you can choose a piece of music in any key, and use five (or more) different key harmonicas to play along with it, each in a different position!

Positions: *First* Definition

Here's a really simple definition of harmonica positions. After we've learned more about music and positions, I'll give you another definition.

Positions tell us about the *relationship* between the key of the music that we are playing, and the key of the harmonica that we are using to play it.

IMPORTANT: Please notice that we can look at positions in **two different ways:** starting with the **Music Key,** or starting with the **Harmonica Key!** Make sure you understand the following sections!

One Key of Music, Many Harmonicas

We can choose *one particular key of music* to play, then see which different harmonicas we can use to play along with that particular key of music, using the different positions. This means that...

When we choose **one particular key of music** to play, positions describe the relationship between:

- The key of the music that we are playing, and...

- the key of the harmonica that we're using to play it..

Examples: When we play music in the key of C, using a key of "C" harmonica — we call that "playing in **First Position.**"

When we play music in the key of C, using a key of "F" harmonica — we call that "playing in **Second Position.**"

When we play music in the key of C, using a key of "Bb" harmonica — we call that "playing in **Third Position.**"

When we play music in the key of C, using a key of "Eb" harmonica — we call that "playing in **Fourth Position.**"

When we play music in the key of C, using a key of "Ab" harmonica — we call that "playing in **Fifth Position.**"

Seven other positions **(Sixth through Twelfth)** exist, but are less commonly used.

Twelve Music Keys Times Twelve Positions

Music in *any* of the twelve possible music keys can be played using these twelve positions. So we can choose to play music in the key of B flat (or C, or E, or any other key), and be able to play along with that key of music using up to *twelve* different key harmonicas (if we're good at playing positions!).

One Harmonica, Many Keys of Music

Or we can choose *one particular key of harmonica* to use, then see which different keys of music that we can play along with, using our one harmonica in different positions. This means that...

When we choose **one particular harmonica** to use, positions can describe the relationship between:

- The key of the harmonica that we have chosen to play, and...

- the different keys of music that we can play with it.

For Example:

When we play a "C" harmonica along with music in the key of C, we call that "playing in **First Position.**"

When we play a "C" harmonica along with music in the key of G, we call that "playing in **Second Position.**"

When we play a "C" harmonica along with music in the key of D, we call that "playing in **Third Position.**"

When we play a "C" harmonica along with music in the key of A, we call that "playing in **Fourth Position.**"

When we play a "C" harmonica along with music in the key of E, we call that "playing in **Fifth Position.**"

Just as I said in the section before this, seven other positions **(Sixth through Twelfth)** exist, but are less commonly used.

Twelve Harp Keys Times Twelve Positions

We can use each of these twelve positions with **any key harmonica,** not just a "C" harmonica.

★★★ IMPORTANT!

Make sure that you really understand the difference between:

- Choosing a particular key of **music** then deciding which **harmonica keys** can play along with that one music key, in the different positions, and...

- Choosing a particular key **harmonica,** then deciding which **music** keys you can play along with — using that one harmonica in many different positions!

How To Play in Positions

Understanding what positions are, and why they work, and how to use them well — is pretty complicated.

Knowing which harmonica to play in what position with which key of music takes either a lot of memorization, or the use of key charts (or the use of my PositionFinder™ Method).

But actually *playing* using positions (at a basic level) is very easy. Most of this information is in Part Two of this book, but here's just a taste, to encourage you.

Different Notes, Same Holes, Same Song

The actual notes on each different key harmonica are different. The 1 out of a C harp is a C note, and the 1 out of a Bb harp is a Bb note. All the rest of the notes are different, too.

But the way that the notes are *arranged* on each harmonica is the same, no matter what the actual notes are. So I can tell you to play the first four notes of the song *Oh When the Saints Go Marchin' In* using the notes 4 out, then 5 out, then 5 in, then 6 out. It doesn't matter what key harmonica you have — the song will come out right!

That's why the following rules work, no matter what key harp you try them on. (As long as you are not playing along with any other musicians — then the key of your harmonica does matter — a lot!)

The Simplest Position Rules

Here, for example, are three unbelievably simple rules that tell you what is "safe" to do in First, Second, or Third Position. If you learn these three rules, the notes you use will always fit in (that's what "safe" means.)

Just play any combinations of the notes that each rule describes. Jump from note to note, slide from note to note, shake it around, use some hand "wah wah," do whatever you like — on just the notes that the rules indicate.

The bad news is that you won't play very exciting stuff — that requires a deeper understanding of positions. But these rules are worth knowing, especially for newer players.

Try each rule now, for a minute — all by yourself. You'll see that each rule helps you to produce notes that sound right together. Why do it by yourself? Because if you want to do it with other musicians or recorded music, you will need to know which key harp to use with which key music, and I haven't gotten around to that (except for the examples I've already given you, which don't cover every key possibility).

The Simplest First Position Rule

• Use any combination of blow notes from hole 1 to hole 10— breathe Out only. Got a "C" harp? Do this while your guitarist plays a C chord.

The Simplest Second Position Rule

• Use any combination of draw notes from hole 1 to hole 5— breathe In only. Got a "C" harp? Do this while your guitarist plays a G or G7 chord.

The Simplest Third Position Rule

• Use any combination of draw notes from hole 4 to hole 10— breathe In only. Got a "C" harp? Do this while your guitarist plays a D chord, or a D Minor Chord or D7. (Don't have a guitar playing friend? My "Positions" tape will stand in for one, but you'll need a key of "A" harmonica.)

Why the Simple Position Rules Work

Why do these simple rules work? Because each rule helps you to use only (or mostly) notes chosen from a certain "scale." That "certain scale" will be the scale that fits well with that position. For example, using the draw notes 4 to 10 gives you lots of notes from "The Third Position Blues Scale." So scales are at the heart of positions, as you will soon learn!

Most experienced harmonica players use First and Second Positions. But I believe that *every* harp player should eventually learn:

• To feel comfortable in First, Second, and Third Positions.

• To be able to use Fourth and Fifth Positions in some situations.

• To "fool around" with at least some of the Sixth through Twelfth Positions.

You can do all of these things, even if you are not an advanced player (try the **"Simple Position Rules,"** above). You don't even need to be able to bend notes (although you should be working on it!).

How to Sound Really Awful!

Using the right "key" harmonica to play in the correct position is super important. It matches our playing to the key of the music that we are playing along with.

When playing by ourselves, it does not really matter what key harmonica we use. But when playing along with other musicians, or even with recorded music, using the "wrong key" harmonica is a disaster! It sounds really awful! My **PositionFinder™ Method** will save you from this problem!

How to Sound Really Good!

Once you've read this book, when the bandleader (or your pal with a guitar) says: "Let's do a Twelve Bar Blues in A!" — you'll know which key harmonica to use. In fact, you'll know that you can use at least five different key harmonicas to play along with that "Blues in A!"

But positions do more than just tell us which key harp to use with which key music — each different position has a very different "feel" to it. So you'll have five different possibilities, depending on your mood, and the "feel" of the song.

Did your pal just lose his day job? You'll pull out a G harp, and play some slow, sad, Third Position Blues. Or is everyone feelin' great, and you want to rock the house? Blow some high, sharp First Position using your A harp.

Only carrying your key of F axe tonight? No problem playing a Blues in A — since you know how to use Fifth Position to play an A Blues with an F harp! Want something even more traditionally mournful than Third Position, using the "Minor" scale? Use your C harp in Fourth Position, and make 'em cry! Or use that old standby Second Position, and blow some D harmonica!

Positions and "Scales"

Why do the different positions have different "feels" to them? Because each position is based on a different **"scale,"** (this is a simplification, but I'll say it for now).

A scale is just a particular combination of notes. The notes of a scale are used to create songs, or riffs, or solos. You are probably already familiar with the most commonly used scale, called the **"Major Scale."** It is sometimes written out like this:

DO   RE   MI   FA   SO   LA   TI   DO

But two other scales, used for Blues and rock music, are even more important to us. Each scale has a different **"feel"** to it, which we'll learn for ourselves, as soon as we can play some!

HarpTab™

In the rest of this book, I'll be writing down lots of harmonica music for you to play. I want to do it in the simplest way possible, so we can try some songs, riffs, and scales, right away!

There are lots of different ways of writing harmonica music. Some, like the lines, spaces, and staffs of standard music notation, are quite difficult to learn.

Other systems, known as "tablature," just tell you which hole to blow through, and which hole to draw through. Some tablature systems use arrows for blow and draw, others use B and D, or In and Out.

I like my system best, with OUTLINED numbers telling you to breathe out, and **FILLED IN** numbers telling you to breathe in. I'll describe it in the box, below.

By the way, I use bits of well known songs here, rather than hot Blues or rock riffs, to demonstrate the notation system. Yes, it's more boring, but at least most of you will know how the song "should sound," which makes figuring out the notation much easier. You'll get to the more exciting stuff soon!

HarpTab™ Basics

I call my simple harmonica notation system HarpTab™. It tells you which holes to breathe in or out on, and how long to do it for. If you have learned my notation before, keep on going. If not, take a minute and learn it right now.

• **The numbers from 1 to 10 tell you which hole of the harmonica to aim your mouth at.**

• **If a number is** OUTLINED, **breathe** OUT. So "4" means breathe <u>out</u> on hole 4.

• **If a number is FILLED IN, breathe IN. So "6" means breathe <u>in</u> on hole 6.**

HarpTab™ Song Examples

Try a few examples to make sure that you've got the idea. In fact, let's use some different positions right now, even if you don't have the faintest idea what a position is! Just play 'em! Here are the first lines of some great songs, in various positions. I'll show you how to figure out the rest of each song by yourself in a minute!

Oh When the Saints (First Position) ★

Oh	when	the	saints	go	mar-	chin'	in
4	5	**5**	6	4	5	**5**	6

Twinkle Twinkle Little Star (First Position) ★

Twin-	kle	twin-	kle	lit-	tle	star
4	4	6	6	**6**	**6**	6

Amazing Grace (First Position) ★

A-	a-	maz-	ing	Grace	how	sweet	the	sound
5	**4**	4	5	5	**4**	**4**	**6**	6

Greensleeves (Fourth Position) ★

A-	las	my	lo-	ove	you	do	me	wrong
6	7	**8**	8	**9**	8	**8**	**7**	6

St. James Infirmary (Fourth Position) ★

Well	I	went	down	to	Saint	James	In-	firm-	ry
6	7	8	8	7	**8**	8	**8**	7	**6**

Why Tablature is Convenient

Tablature systems are very convenient for harmonica players. Why? Because if we used any type of "standard musical notation," which uses the letter names for each note, we would have to write a song using different letter names for each key harmonica. The first four notes of *Oh When the Saints* would be C - E - F - G on your key of C harmonica, and Gb - Bb - B - Db on your key of Gb harmonica! In tablature, it's *always* 4 - 5 - 5 - 6, no matter which key harmonica you have!

About Single Notes

You're going to need to be able to get single notes if you want to use positions. I think the easiest way to get single notes is to make a small hole with your lips, as though you were whistling. Then just aim your "lip hole" at the harmonica hole that you want to get. Pucker up!

If you are already using the more difficult single note method known as "tongue blocking," that's okay with me. It may be harder to learn to bend notes if you tongue block than if you "pucker."

Scales and Songs

Scales. They sound boring, like something that your third grade piano teacher tried to make you play. But knowing what scales are and how to use them is at the heart of making Blues and rock music, especially if you want to create your own riffs, songs, and solos.

- **Scales** are groups of notes that are used as the "building blocks" for songs. There are really only four scales that harmonica players need to know about.

- There is a very important scale used for Blues and rock music, called the **"Blues Scale."**

- There's a scale for rock music and for country & western music, called the **"Country Pentatonic Scale."** It's sometimes used in Blues, too.

- There are also two other scales, used for folk, classical, and popular music.

- The **"Major Scale"** is used more for "happy" or "upbeat" folk and pop music.

- The **"Minor Scale"** is used more for "sad" music, and for Eastern European style music, like the plaintive sounding music of the Gypsy and Jewish peoples.

Scales: Musical Alphabets?

In a way, we might consider a "scale" to be a kind of **"musical alphabet"**. How's that? Well, by using various combinations of the 26 letters of the English alphabet we create English words, sentences, paragraphs and books. By using the letters of the Russian alphabet we create Russian words, sentences and long dreary novels.

Likewise, the notes of any particular scale — Blues Scale, Country Scale, Major Scale or Minor Scale — can be put together in various combinations and rhythms to create music with a very particular "feel."

Letter Names of Scales

> Whenever we choose a note to begin a scale on, the letter name of that beginning note is called the **"key"** of that scale.

So the Major Scale beginning on the note G is called a **G Major Scale,** or a **Major Scale in the key of G.**

The Minor Scale beginning on the note **B** is called a **B Minor Scale,** or a **Minor Scale in the key of B.**

The Blues Scale beginning on the note **Eb (E flat)** is called an **Eb Blues Scale,** or a **Blues Scale in the key of Eb.**

The same is true for any type of scale. It will always be named after the letter name of the note that it starts on.

What Key is the Music In?

> If we know what scale was used to create a piece of music, we also know the key of that piece of music. Use a D Minor scale to compose or improvise your music, and that music will be "in the key of D Minor." Use an A Major scale to compose or improvise another piece, and that piece will be "in the key of A Major."

When composing using the Blues or Pentatonic Scale, just the key is usually used to name the music. So a piece created from the Eb Blues Scale is said simply to be "in the key of Eb." The Blues speaks for itself!

So when the bandleader says, let's play a Blues in the key of F, you know what to do. You've got to play using a Blues Scale in the key of F. But there are lots of different ways — and positions — to do this!

> If you ever want to play with a band, or other musicians, read this section.

Using Scales to Create Songs

It's not too difficult to use scales to create a song. First we decide what kind of a song we want to play. Is it a Blues song, or a rock song? Country or folk? Does it have a happy or a sad feeling?

Our answers to these questions help to tell us which scale we are going to use. Then we chose combinations of notes from that scale to produce the song.

Let's learn to play some easy scales — scales that are "built in" to the harmonica. Then we'll look at how those scales provide the notes for songs that we already know. Doing this will help us to make up our own songs, riffs, and solos, later on. Knowing these scales will also help us be able to figure out songs that are based on these scales.

Two "Built-In" Scales

The notes on your ten hole harmonica are arranged to make it easy to play two scales: a Major Scale in the middle of the harmonica, and a Minor Scale up towards the high end. Here's how it happened.

The First Modern Harmonica

About 180 years ago, the first harmonica was invented in Germany. Early harmonicas had varying numbers of holes (up to 20 or so), and various ways of arranging the notes (musical sounds) within those holes.

But by the late 1830's an instrument maker named Richter had created a harmonica remarkably similar to the one we know today. It had ten holes, and could produce a sound on the in breath and the out breath. More importantly, the way that the notes were arranged in the ten little holes was the same as it is today.

German Folk Music Made Easy

Herr Richter arranged the notes the way he did for a very specific purpose. He wanted to make it easy to play European folk and classical music on the harmonica.

As you now know, the Major and Minor Scales are the "musical alphabets"of most European folk and classical music.

So Herr Richter arranged the notes of the harmonica so that it would be easy to play Major and Minor scales on the instrument.

For example, the C Major and A Minor Scales can be played very easily on the key of C ten hole harmonica. It is very clear that Herr Richter intended the player with a key of C harmonica to play mainly using the scales of C Major and A Minor.

In order to do this, he had to leave certain notes out of the harmonica. In fact, the harmonica is missing quite a few notes. That's one of the reasons we have to learn to "bend" notes — to supply the missing ones!

About The Major Scale

The Major Scale tends to have a strong, brassy, bouncy feel to it. Even random playing of the Major Scale notes sounds good to us — because these notes are the most basic building blocks of our American musical heritage. Lots of American folk music (and most of our classical music) comes from Europe, so we will use the Major Scale quite a bit, if we play folk or classical music.

Many different Major Scales can be played on the harmonica, but here is by far the easiest one — built right into the harmonica! Play it, now!

The First Position Major Scale ★

4̲ **4** 5̲ **5** 6̲ **6** **7** 7̲

I call this scale the **"Mid-Range First Position Major Scale."** Where does that name come from? Mid-range, since these notes are in the middle of the harmonica. And First Position? I'm not sure where that name came from, but that's what we call it. I'll discuss "position names" more, later.

Now look at the notes used in some songs that are based on the Major Scale. You can see that these songs use Major Scale notes as their "building blocks," or "musical alphabet."

Oh	when	the	saints	go	mar-	chin'	in
4̲	5̲	**5**	6̲	4̲	5̲	**5**	6̲

Twin-	kle	twin-	kle	lit-	tle	star
4̲	**4**	6̲	6̲	**6**	**6**	6̲

A-	a-	maz-	ing	Grace	how	sweet	the	sound
5̲	**4**	4̲	5̲	5̲	**4**	**4**	**6**	6̲

Practice playing the Major Scale for a minute, then try using it. Figure out the rest of the songs, above, using just notes from the Major Scale. Or see if you can put some of the notes together in any combination, to compose your own First Position Major Scale song. It doesn't have to sound great — just experiment. And figure out how to play some of your other favorite folk melodies, right now!

About The Minor Scale

The Minor Scale has a more plaintive or wistful quality than the Major Scale. Here is the easiest Minor Scale on the harmonica. A number of other Minor Scales are also possible. This one can be called the **"High End Fourth Position Minor Scale:"**

The Fourth Position Minor Scale ★

6 **7** 7̲ **8** 8̲ **9** 9̲ **10**

Look at the notes used in these Fourth Position arrangements of *Greensleeves* and *St. James Infirmary.* You can easily see how the Minor Scale was used as their "musical alphabet!" Can you play the rest of each tune?

A-	las	my	lo-	ove	you	do	me	wrong
6	7̃	8	8̃	9	8̃	8	7	6̃

Well	I	went	down	to	Saint	James	In-	firm-	ry
6	7̃	8̃	8̃	7̃	8	8̃	8	7̃	6

Practice playing the Minor Scale for a minute, then try figuring out some other Fourth Position Minor songs, like *Summertime* (begins on 8 out) or *Autumn Leaves* (begins on 6 in). Put some of the notes together in any combination, to compose a Fourth Position Minor song — Experiment!

There are a number of variations of the minor scale. The above one is most commonly used, and called the **Natural Minor** or **Aeolian Minor** Scale.

The other most common Minor Scale variation is called the **Dorian Minor Scale,** and we'll learn it when we get to Third Position. **Third Position** is also great for playing Blues, especially slow, sad, Blues — since we can easily *combine* the Minor and the Blues Scale!

The Earliest Positions

I don't know when the term "position" first came to be used. Certainly Mr. Richter, in the 1830's, did not use that word to describe his "built in" Major and Minor Scales. But it wouldn't be wrong to say that these two scales were the earliest positions: First Position, and Fourth Position.

Make sure that you can play the scales that are "built in" to the harmonica. They are the **First Position Major Scale** and the **Fourth Position Minor Scale** written above. And see how the notes of these two scales are used in the song examples I've given you.

I'll be giving you lots more Major, Minor, Blues, and Pentatonic Scales for the other positions, in Part Two. So make sure you understand what scales are, and how they're used. And for lots more songs in HarpTab, see *The Pocket Harmonica Songbook,* page 94.

Bending and Scales

As I said earlier, the ten hole harmonica is not your normal instrument. Many of the musical notes that we would expect to find in it don't seem to exist at all. Don't exist, that is, until we discover "bending."

Bending notes allows us to play notes and scales that are not "built in" to the harmonica. The good news is that with bending, we can play lots of scales that we could not otherwise use. The bad news is that some of them are hard!

If you're sure already know what bending is, you can skip the next section. If not...

A Confession

This was a hard section for me to write. If you're already a good bender, this may be boring. If you can't bend at all, it'll be a tease, since it talks *about* bending, but probably won't give you enough to learn *how* to bend, and you may just feel like I'm trying to sell you another book.

But if you can bend some — or think that you can, but aren't sure if you're doing it right — this section will give you enough to play the bending scales and exercises in the first half of the book.

What is Bending?

> Bending a note means making the note sound *lower* than it normally does, by blocking part of the airway with your tongue. It's a lovely, growly, gutsy sound.

Bending requires good single noting ability. It also requires lots of tongue control, since you must pull your tongue back and down into your mouth to find the exact spot that produces a bend. And that exact spot is different for each note of each different key harmonica. Plus, some holes can be bent down to produce not one but two or even three extra notes! Here are two diagrams from my *Bending the Blues*, showing the approximate tongue placement for bent (right) and unbent (left) notes.

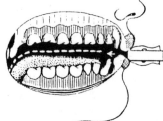 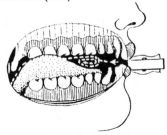

One Hole, Three Half Step Bends?

Remember "half steps" (page 10)? Some notes — like the 1 in, 4 in, 5 in, and 6 in — can only be bent down one half step to the "b" bend. Other notes, like 2 in, can be bent down one half step to the "b" or two half steps down to the "bb." And the note 3 in can be bent to three different bends: "b" (one half step) and "bb" (two half steps) and "bbb" (three half steps) — which makes it a tricky one!

HarpTab™ Bending Notation

> • If a number is followed by one or two or three little "b" symbols, it needs to be "bent." The number of "b's" tells you how far to bend. One "b" is the least bent, and three "bbb" is the most bent. Only one hole, the 3 in, can be bent to the "bbb."
>
> • Later on I'll give you some harder examples, with overblows and other hard stuff. But for now, we'll only be using a single "b" bend on holes 3 and 4 in.

Bending is essential for Blues playing, and very useful for every other style of playing, since it provides notes that are not otherwise on the standard tuned harmonica. But luckily for those of us that can't bend yet, nothing in Part One, and many of the scales, songs, exercises, riffs, and solos in Part Two, won't require bending.

HarpTab™ Bending Examples

If you can "kind of" bend, here are some easy song examples, to help you perfect your bends and use my bending notation. If you can't bend yet, you'll need more help than this, so don't feel bad about not being able to play these examples. Just get used to the notation!

Finding the 3b Bend

Playing either the first line of *Greensleeves* (in Second Position, which is actually rarely used for this song) or *Saint James Infirmary* (in Second Position, which is often used for this song) will help you to hear and find the 3 in note which is bent to the "b" bend. That's the 3 in bend used in the first Blues Scale that we will study.

Notice that if you don't bend the 3 in, the song sounds wrong. It also sounds wrong if you "bend the note too far" (like to the "bb" or "bbb" bend). If this seems too confusing — sorry, you need *Bending the Blues* (page 94).

A-	las	my	lo-	ve
2	**3b**	**4**	**4**	

Well	I	went	down	to	Saint	James	In-	firm-	ary
2	**3b**	**4**	**4**	**3b**	**4**	**4**	**4**	**3b**	**2**

Finding the 4b Bend

In some ways, finding the 4 in "b" bend is easier than finding the 3 in "b" bend. That's because the "b" bend is the only bend you can get out of the note 4 in. The only mistake you can make is not being able to bend it at all!

Playing just the first three notes of *Joy to the World* (in Third Position) will help you to hear and find the 4 in "b" bend (the rest of the line requires harder bends).

Joy	to	the	(world	the	Lord	has	come)
4	**4b**	**3**	**(3bb**	**2**	**2b**	**2**	**1)**

The "Dwah" — An Easy Bend Effect

> I often like you to add a slight or very rapid bend to begin a note. In other words, you hit the note slightly bent, then release it almost instantly.

I notate this with a "**dwah.**" The "dw-" sound represents the bend on the note, and the "-ah" sound the release of the bend. Do it with your lips in *tight single note shape!*

Simply whispering a *very* clear and *very* forceful "dwah" through a *single* hole (on in or out breath) should produce a slightly bent tone. It's not as good as a real bend, but better than nothing! Use it on any note with a "b" bend notation, if you can't bend. Try a Fourth Position example:

Well	I	went	down	to	Saint	James	In-	firm-	ary
dwah		dwah	dwah			dwah			dwah
6	**7**	**8**	**8**	**7**	**8**	**8**	**8**	**7**	**6**

Can't get a good sound? Check out *Bending the Blues*...

About the Blues

The harmonica came to America in a big way during the Civil War, exported by the Hohner Company. And after that war, many of the former slaves, most of whom came originally from the West coast of Africa, began to pick up the most inexpensive and portable instrument that the world had ever known.

The kind of music that many of these African-American musicians chose to play was quite different than European folk and classical music. Their music was of a more vocal and improvisational tradition, with strong emphasis on rhythm and emotion.

The notes that they chose to sing and play had a plaintive air, in between the notes of the Major and Minor Scales. Some of the notes were not even played to an exact pitch, but were slurred and wailed. These notes could be easily sung, but were impossible to play on an instrument like a piano — they fell into the cracks between the keys!

This type of music could not be easily played using the Major Scale that the harmonica was created to play. And, over time, a new scale evolved. It had a wistful feel, fewer notes than the Major or Minor Scales, and some of those slurred, wailed notes from the cracks between the keys of the piano. And the "Blues Scale" was born. Perhaps its creators didn't think of it as a scale at all — but that's what it turned out to be.

> No one knows exactly when, or how, or where, it happened. But somehow a new style of music — using a unique structure of chords and a new scale — emerged in the South of the United States, somewhere around the turn of the century. This music combined the African musical tradition with the European musical tradition.
>
> The chord structure (which we will learn to play soon) was called **"The Twelve Bar Blues Structure."** The new scale was our **"Blues Scale."** Together, they added up to: **The Blues.**
>
> Over time, many new styles of music came out of The Blues and the Blues Scale. Rock and roll, R & B, and lots of country and jazz songs are directly based on The Blues! Why do I capitalize The Blues? As a sign of well-deserved respect!

The Blues Scale

So the mingling of the European musical tradition with the African musical tradition resulted in the creation of the Afro-American **Blues Scale.** Its six notes always sound "Bluesy" when played together in any combination.

There are many ways and many positions in which you can play Blues Scales on the harmonica. Some are easier (none are too easy, since they all require bending), and some are much harder.

An Unknown Genius

By the 1930's (and maybe long before, unrecorded), a new style of playing had revolutionized the world of harmonica. Some unknown genius had tried playing music using this new and excitingly different scale on the harmonica.

This genius decided not to play the built in Major and Minor Scales that were usually used. Instead, he or she began to play notes that belonged to a scale that would, eventually, stretch between the 2 in and the 6 out.

Cross Harp

Perhaps it started as an accident. But African-American harmonica players discovered that by playing this way, you could more easily produce a Bluesy feel. And a beautiful, strange, powerful effect called "bending" could slur and wail some of the notes.

This new style of playing caught on, from the Mississippi Delta to Chicago. As it became more popular, it became more standardized as well, and the modern harmonica Blues Scale came into being.

As the technique of bending developed, this Blues Scale could be played anywhere on the harmonica. But the easiest place to get this full scale (called the **"Mid-Range Second Position** or **'Cross' Blues Scale."**) was between holes 2 and 6, like this.

The Second Position Blues Scale ★★

2   3b   4̸   4b   4   5   ⑥

Eventually this type of playing came to be known as **"Cross"** harp, or **"Second Position."** Just as with any scale written in tablature, once you learn this Blues Scale you can use it on any key harmonica. Play it from 2 in up to 6 out, then going down, from 6 out to 2 in.

If you can't bend notes yet (as notated by the little b symbols), don't worry — there are lots of great things to do with this scale even for "pre-benders! Just try a simplified version, playing up, then down. Dwah it!

The Simplified Second Position Blues Scale ★

dwah   dwah

2   3   4̸   4   4   5   ⑥

> The **Blues Scale** is at the heart of Blues and rock music. It provides us with the **"musical alphabet"** for Blues and rock music. Play the **Second Position Blues Scale** above a few times, even if you have to fudge the bends. Even if you already know it. In fact, why don't you read this whole section!

Other Position Blues Scales

Blues Scales are also available in many other positions. The Blues Scale of each position sounds a bit different, since the bent notes fall in different places. After we learn how to use the Second Position Blues Scale, we'll learn some others, too — easy ones, and hard.

The Third and First Position Blues Scales are the next most important after the Second Position Blues Scale, then come the Fourth and Fifth Position Blues Scales. And there are seven more after that, of course!

Using the Cross Blues Scale

Before we go on to other positions, let's look at how riffs and solos are created from the Blues Scale. In order to do this, I'll need to define a few new terms, and teach you a timing notation system for HarpTab™.

Composition and Improvisation

When we play a song that has been written down, we are playing a "composition." The song that we are playing has been **"composed,"** which means that the notes were first chosen, then written down for others to play. Composition is often a slow, thoughtful, process, like writing a story or a poem.

But composition is not the only way to make music. Sometimes we create music "on the spot" — that is, making it up as we go. The music just comes out, *while* we are playing. This is called **"improvisation."** Improvisation is often a fast, spontaneous, process — without too much thinking involved. It's more like dancing, or telling a story that we are making up as we go.

> There are two main ways to make music: composition (written down) and improvisation (made up as we go). Either way, we mostly choose the notes that we use from a scale.

Composing and Improvising with Scales

If we want, for instance, to compose or improvise Blues music — we've got to learn to make tasteful combinations of the six notes of the Afro-American **Blues Scale.** This produces music with a "Bluesy" feel.

It's the same for any other scale. If we want to create music with an Eastern European "feel" (like the music of the Gypsy or Jewish peoples), we will use different combinations of notes chosen from the **Minor Scale.**

If we want to create music with a bright, bouncy folk "feel," we will use the notes of the **Major Scale.**

If we want to create C & W music, we'll use a scale — the **Pentatonic Scale** — that produces country music. We'll learn it, soon.

Riffs, Licks, and Solos

> **"Riffs"** (and **"licks"**) are just Blues, rock, and country style music terms that refer to short combinations of notes that we memorize. Both words mean pretty much the same thing. Riffs are created from notes of the Blues or Country Scales.

A riff or a lick is usually from two to sixteen beats long. Often, a good riff is used in *lots* of different songs. For example, both Muddy Waters "Hoochie Coochie Man" and Sonny Boy Williamson II's "Don't Start Me to Talking" use the same wonderful riff , as do dozens more songs. I'll give you that riff soon, in different positions!

A **"Solo"** is a musical term that can be used two ways. It could mean "playing by yourself" — no other musicians.

> But often Blues, rock, jazz, and country musicians use **"solo"** to mean a long combination of notes (longer than a riff) that one musician plays while other musicians are providing a background accompaniment for the "soloist." In Blues music, a solo is often 48 beats long — one "Twelve Bar Blues Verse." But we'll get to that too, soon.

Once we've learned about timing notation, we can start playing riffs and solos of our own, to demonstrate all this.

HarpTab™: Timing

If you've ever tapped your foot while listening to a piece of music, you know that the **"beat"** is the steady pulse that underlies a piece of music. If you know the songs (like *Twinkle Twinkle Little Star*) from the earlier sections, you could probably play them without any kind of timing notation. But when we get to the riffs and solos, you'll need to know what the rhythm is!

I use a dot placed above a note to show you where to tap your foot, that is, where the beat should fall.

> • A dot above a note tells you to **tap your foot** as that note begins.
>
> • If a note must be held for **more than one beat,** there will be more than one dot above it. If three beats are above a note or chord, hold it for all three beats.
>
> • A dot without a note or chord under it represents a **beat of silence.** Tap your foot, but don't play anything.

Try an example, with timing dots. Of course, you may have a slightly different idea of where beats should fall than I do. Play it my way, and yours! My timing dots just suggest the rhythm that sounds best (or sometimes easiest) to me. Notice the two timing variations below. One gives you two silent beats to breathe in, the other doesn't.

Oh	when	the	saints		go	mar-	chin'	in
4̶	5̶	5	6̶		4̶	5̶	5	6̶

Twin- kle twin- kle lit- tle star
4 **4** **6** **6** **6** **6** **6**

Fran- kie and John- nie were lov- ers
2 **3** **4** **5** **4** **3** **2** **2**

Half a Beat is Better than None

> • A note without a dot above it is a note that falls *in between* **two foot taps,** or beats. Since it falls between beats, naturally it last for less than a beat.

Some people would prefer to see *Frankie and Johnnie* written with only half as many dots. Try it this way, though it's a bit harder to read, if you don't know the song. On the plus side, it may have a bouncier feeling, especially if you hit the notes right under each dot a bit harder.

By the way — I often write a riff or solo (or song) using more dots than it would normally have, the first time I write it for you — to make it easier to read.

Fran- kie and John- nie were lov- ers
2 **3** **4** **5** **4** **3** **2** **2**

A folk or classical musician seeing this would give each note *Fran* and *kie*, and *John* and *nie* exactly one-half a beat each.

Swing Time

> Blues musicians, seeing this notation, might want to **"swing"** the beat, which means holding the note that begins right on the beat (like the *Fran*, which is under the dot) for a little longer than the note which follows and which does not begin on the beat (like the *kie*, which isn't under a dot).
>
> Sometimes the "dot note" gets two thirds of the beat, and the "no dot note" gets one third. And sometimes, the "dot note" gets three quarters of the beat, and the "no dot note" gets only one quarter.

I can indicate a suggested swing beat by making the note that gets played less long a little smaller, like this:

Fran- kie and John- nie were lov- ers
2 3 **4** **5** 4 **3** **2** **2**

Jazzy Frankie and Johnnie

Sometimes trying it with more dots will help you get the jazzy swing feel, called a "jazz triplet swing" timing (two thirds/one third):

●●	●	●●●	●●	●	●●●	●●●	●●●	●●●	●●●
Fran-	kie	and	John-	nie	were	lov-	ers		
2	3	**4**	5̲	4	**3**	**2**	**2**		

Swingin' "Boogie Woogie"

This easy Second Position "boogie woogie" or "Blues shuffle" riff also uses swing timing.

•		•		•	
2	2	**3**	3	**4**	4

•		•	•	•	•
5̲	5̲	**5**	4	5̲	**4**

Try "more dot" notation, if the first one was hard to read.

••	•	••	•	••	•
2	2	**3**	3	**4**	4

••	•	••	•	●●●	●●●	●●●
5̲	5̲	**5**	4	5̲	**4**	

Sometimes, if *all* the notes in a song are swing beats, I will just tell you to swing the beat in the instructions at the beginning of the song. Then you'll just hold the notes that fall *under* dots a bit longer than the notes that fall *in between* dots. Get it?

Riffs from The Blues Scale

This is not a book of riffs (though I am working on one). But I want you to be able to play at least a few riffs in all of the most important positions (and a few of the oddball ones, as well!). Even more importantly, I want you to understand how riffs are created from scales, so that you can use the material in Part Two to make up riffs of your own, for every position! Most of the riffs that I give you are pretty simple in rhythm and note use, so you can concentrate on getting the scales and positions down!

So now that you can read timing notation, try playing the riff I discussed before, used in *"Hoochie Coochie"* and *"Don't Start Me to Talkin'"* Blues songs. I will use this lovely riff as an example in many different positions, so get used to it!

Creating Riffs from the Blues Scale

I've already demonstrated how certain types of songs (like *Twinkle Twinkle Little Star,* and *Greensleeves*) are created from notes of the Major or Minor Scales (page 20).

> Blues riffs are created using notes from the Blues Scale. You'll notice in a moment that all of the notes of the *"Hoochie Talk"* riff are taken directly from the second half of the Second Position Blues Scale:

2 3ᵇ 4̸ 4ᵇ 4 5 ⑥

The Second Position *"Hoochie Talk"* Riff ★

We might call this the basic **Second Position "Hoochie Talk" Riff**. Here it is, with three times as many dots as you'll end up with, to help you get the rhythm. Count out those seven silent beats at then end, then repeat it. Start slow, then speed it up.

•   •   •   •   •   •••   ••••
4   5   4   5   ⑥

Now try it with only a third as many dots (remember to tap much slower this way, or you'll play it too fast). Emphasize the notes that fall under each dot just a bit. Often, a singer will use the two silent beats to sing in.

•   •   •   •   •
4   5   4   5   ⑥

You can swing the beat some, if you like.

•   •   •   •
4   5   4   5   ⑥

Don't Got That Swing?

If you don't have the hang of swinging the beat, try this:

•   ••   •   •   ••••   •••
4   5   4   5   ⑥

More Blues Scale Riffs

We can compose some new Blues riffs by choosing notes from the Blues Scale, and adding some kind of timing rhythm that feels right to us. Now we'll use the same rhythm as the "Hoochie Talk" riff, but choose new notes.

Here's another riff (*"Hoochie Talk #2"*), using notes chosen from low end of the Second Position Blues Scale. If you can't bend yet, just "dwah" the heck out of each 3 in "b."

"Hoochie Talk Riff #2" ★ or ★★

•   •   •   •   •   •••   ••••
2   3ᵇ   4̸   3ᵇ   4

Now try it with only a third as many dots.

•   •   •   •
2   3ᵇ   4̸   3ᵇ   4

You can swing the beat some or not, as you like.

•   •   •
2   3ᵇ   4̸   3ᵇ   4

Here's one more riff ("*Hoochie Talk #3*"), also from the notes of the Second Position Blues Scale.

"*Hoochie Talk* Riff #3 ★ or ★★

$\overset{\bullet}{5}$ $\overset{\bullet}{4}$ $\overset{\bullet}{4}$ $\overset{\bullet}{3_b}$ $\overset{\bullet}{2}$ ●●● ●●●●

Now try it with only a third as many dots.

5 $\overset{\bullet}{4}$ 4 3_b $\overset{\bullet}{2}$ ● ●

Swing the beat some, if you want.

5 $\overset{\bullet}{4}$ 4 3_b $\overset{\bullet}{2}$ ● ●

Now we'll put some riffs together to create a longer piece of music: a solo!

"*Hoochie Talk*" Solo #1 ★ or ★★

We can do two versions of this same solo. Our first version will just alternate the original riff with the new ones. I'll use simple (more dots) timing, to help you see how the riffs fit together.

$\overset{\bullet}{4}$ $\overset{\bullet}{5}$ $\overset{\bullet}{4}$ $\overset{\bullet}{5}$ $\overset{\bullet}{⑥}$ ●●● ●●●●

$\overset{\bullet}{2}$ $\overset{\bullet}{3_b}$ $\overset{\bullet}{4}$ $\overset{\bullet}{3_b}$ $\overset{\bullet}{4}$ ●●● ●●●●

$\overset{\bullet}{4}$ $\overset{\bullet}{5}$ $\overset{\bullet}{4}$ $\overset{\bullet}{5}$ $\overset{\bullet}{⑥}$ ●●● ●●●●

$\overset{\bullet}{5}$ $\overset{\bullet}{4}$ $\overset{\bullet}{4}$ $\overset{\bullet}{3_b}$ $\overset{\bullet}{2}$ ●●● ●●●●

$\overset{\bullet}{4}$ $\overset{\bullet}{5}$ $\overset{\bullet}{4}$ $\overset{\bullet}{5}$ $\overset{\bullet}{⑥}$ ●●● ●●●●

Now try reading it with the actual timing. It should sound the same, but bouncier.

4 $\overset{\bullet}{5}$ 4 5 $\overset{\bullet}{⑥}$ ● ●

2 $\overset{\bullet}{3_b}$ 4 3_b $\overset{\bullet}{4}$ ● ●

4 $\overset{\bullet}{5}$ 4 5 $\overset{\bullet}{⑥}$ ● ●

5 $\overset{\bullet}{4}$ 4 3_b $\overset{\bullet}{2}$ ● ●

4 $\overset{\bullet}{5}$ 4 5 $\overset{\bullet}{⑥}$ ● ●

"Hoochie Talk" Solo #2 ★ or ★★

Our second version will "sandwich" the new riffs into the silences of the first riff. Here's what it looks like, with simplified timing dots. Practice to get the timing, especially when going from one line to the next.

$$\overset{\bullet}{4} \quad \overset{\bullet}{5} \quad \overset{\bullet}{4} \quad \overset{\bullet}{5} \quad \overset{\bullet}{\textcircled{6}} \quad \overset{\bullet}{}$$

$$\overset{\bullet}{2} \quad \overset{\bullet}{3b} \quad \overset{\bullet}{\textit{4}} \quad \overset{\bullet}{3b} \quad \overset{\bullet}{4} \quad \overset{\bullet}{}$$

$$\overset{\bullet}{4} \quad \overset{\bullet}{5} \quad \overset{\bullet}{4} \quad \overset{\bullet}{5} \quad \overset{\bullet}{\textcircled{6}} \quad \overset{\bullet}{}$$

$$\overset{\bullet}{5} \quad \overset{\bullet}{4} \quad \overset{\bullet}{\textit{4}} \quad \overset{\bullet}{3b} \quad \overset{\bullet}{2} \quad \overset{\bullet}{}$$

$$\overset{\bullet}{4} \quad \overset{\bullet}{5} \quad \overset{\bullet}{4} \quad \overset{\bullet}{5} \quad \overset{\bullet}{\textcircled{6}} \quad \overset{\bullet}{}$$

And with the actual timing dots, it will sound almost the same, but bouncier:

$$4 \quad \overset{\bullet}{5} \quad 4 \quad 5 \quad \overset{\bullet}{\textcircled{6}}$$

$$2 \quad \overset{\bullet}{3b} \quad \textit{4} \quad 3b \quad \overset{\bullet}{4}$$

$$4 \quad \overset{\bullet}{5} \quad 4 \quad 5 \quad \overset{\bullet}{\textcircled{6}}$$

$$5 \quad \overset{\bullet}{4} \quad \textit{4} \quad 3b \quad \overset{\bullet}{2}$$

$$4 \quad \overset{\bullet}{5} \quad 4 \quad 5 \quad \overset{\bullet}{\textcircled{6}}$$

"Hoochie Talk" Longest Solo #3 ★ or ★★

For a long solo, play Solo #1, then (without a break) #2, then #1 again.

Note: If you are playing using the "more dots" notation for Solo #1, you must do the same on #2, or your timing will not be consistent.

Or if you are playing using the "actual dots" notation for Solo #1, you must do the same on #2.

A Playalong Hint: These "Hoochie Talk" Solos work fine when played on harmonica only. Later on, if you try to fit them in to the Twelve Bar Blues, you will find that you have to start playing the riff one beat before you start the actual Twelve Bar. But don't worry about this unless you plan to play these solos along with other musicians...

> **Important:** Make sure that you understand how riffs are created using the notes of the Blues Scale, as I describe and demonstrate above. We'll be doing this with lots of different scales in different positions, in Part Two.

The Blues Scale as Riff

> By adding some rhythm, the Blues Scale itself can make a great riff. We'll be using this kind of Blues Scale Riff a lot in Part Two, in all of the different positions — so make sure that you understand these examples.

Here are some of my favorite Blues Scale Riffs, each eight beats long, using the Second Position Blues Scale. If you can't bend, just use "dwah" on the 3 in and 4 in for the 3 in bent and 4 in bent notes. It won't sound as good, but it will work! And *keep working* on your bending!

Blues Scale Riffs ★ or ★★

2 3b 4 4b 4 5 ⑥ •

2 3b 4 4b 4 5 ⑥ •

2 3b 4 4b 4 5 ⑥ •

⑥ 5 4 4b 4 3b 2 •

⑥ 5 4 4b 4 3b 2 •

⑥ 5 4 4b 4 3b 2

Many Ways to Play Scales

All of the scales that I just discussed can be played on the harmonica. In fact, all of them can be played in much more than one way on the harmonica. Some can be played in dozens of different ways — easier ways, and harder ways. This will be easier to talk about after you've learned more about letter names, and about octave notes.

Octave Notes and Scales

Before I can give you a really good definition of position, and show you some neat ways to play additional Major and Minor Scales on the harmonica, we need to cover the subject of "octaves" and "octave notes." If you already understand this important musical subject, you can skim this chapter.

Consider the Keyboard

Look at the keys of the piano. Don't worry much about the black keys, for now. Notice that each of the white keys has a letter name, from A to G.

You can see that these letter names *repeat themselves* every seven white keys (counting the note that you started on).

In my picture (looking from left to right), these keys go from C to B, then C to B again, then C to B once more. I end my diagram with one last C. So the diagram contains *three* repeated patterns of notes in it (plus the extra C note).

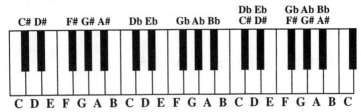

Octave Notes

Notes that have the same letter name are called **"octave notes."** Even though some are higher and some are lower, they somehow sound very much the same. All the C notes sound similar to each other, all the D notes sound similar to each other, all the E notes sound similar to each other, and so on.

The "Octave Distance"

The distance between any two closest octave notes is called "one octave distance," or just one "octave." So from C to the next C is one octave, from A to the next A is one octave, and so on. My keyboard diagram contained three octaves, each one beginning and ending on the note C.

The ten hole harmonica, just like these keyboard diagrams, also contains three octaves. Here is how the notes of a "C harmonica" are arranged. (Outlined = Out notes.)

1	2	3	4	5	6	7	8	9	10
D	G	B	D	F	A	B	D	F	A
C	E	G	C	E	G	C	E	G	C

You can see the notes that Herr Richter left out: two in the low octave, and one in the high octave. He also threw in an extra "G" in the low octave. This extra and missing notes made it easier to play "chords" (multiple notes).

Octaves on the Harp

Play some of these octave note groups on your harp. No matter what key harp you have, the notes in each group should sound similar to each other, just higher or lower.

1	4	7	10		1	4	8
2	3	6	9			2	5	8
5	9			**6**	10		3	7

Now demonstrate some octave distances for yourself on the harmonica by jumping carefully from one octave note to the next highest, for example 1 out to 4 out, or 3 in to 7 in. Being able to jump with accuracy from one octave note to another is very helpful for playing composed music or improvising. It it seems hard, practice!

Missing Note Major Scales

If the note 1 out is the same as the note 4 out, why not play a Major Scale down in the low end? Why not play a Major Scale starting up on the 7 out? No reason — except that certain notes are missing. X marks the spots!

1   1   2   **x**   2   **x**   3   4

7   8   8   9   9   10   **x**   10

Some New First Position Major Scales ★

By leaping from one octave to another (to avoid missing notes), we can play a number of new First Position Major Scales, like these.

1   1   2   5   6   6   3   4

7   8   8   9   9   10   7   7

1   1   2   5   6   6   7   7

4   4   5   5   6   6   3   4

Try some that go from higher to lower, too.

7   7   6   6   5   2   1   1

10   7   6   6   5   5   4   4

Important Major Scale!!! ★

The following scale is expecially useful if you find yourself running into those missing notes in the low end — just jump up and find 'em in the middle!

4   3   6   6   5   5   4   4

For example, to play the song *Amazing Grace* in the mid-range of the harmonica, you must either bend in a 3 in bb note or jump up to the 6 in.

A-	a-	maz-	ing	Grace	how	sweet	the	sound
5	4	4	5	5	4	4	6	6

Songs and Octave Scales

You can use the alternate octave scales to play songs, just as you would use the original scale (as long as you don't run into the missing notes, which is often a big problem with the low end scales if you are not a good bender). Try to figure out the rest of these songs, using the high end Major Scale, which I've written here for your practicing convenience. Play the scale a few times before trying to figure out the songs.

7 8 8 9 9 10 x 10

Oh	when	the	saints	go	mar-	chin'	in
7	8	9	9	7	8	9	9

Twin-	kle	twin-	kle	lit-	tle	star
7	7	9	9	10	10	9

Missing Note Minor Scales

Those same darn missing notes make it hard to play the Fourth Position Minor Scale down lower on the harp! But once again, by leaping from one octave to another, we can avoid the missing notes and play some new Fourth Position Minor Scales.

New Fourth Position Minor Scales ★

6 3 4 4 5 5 6 6

6 7 7 4 5 5 6 6

Or, from higher to lower:

6 6 5 5 4 4 3 6

Missing Note Blues Scales

We already know that we need to bend notes if we want to play a "real" Second Position Blues Scale. But we can easily play a higher octave variation of the Simplified Second Position Blues Scale!

Simplified Second Position Blues Scale ★

    dwah   dwah
2 3 4 4 4 5 6

High, Simple Second Position Blues Scale★

    dwah   dwah
6 7 7 8 8 9 9

We can even "mix and match" the two above scales, to make a new one:

High/Mid Second Position Blues Scale ★

⑥ 7   7̄   4   4   5   ⑥

(dwah over 7, dwah over 7̄)

"Octave" notes are notes that sound the same. They always have the same letter name.

Important: Make sure that you can play some First Position Major Scales, Fourth Position Minor Scales, and Second Position Blues Scales using different octave notes.

Most scales — Major or Minor, Blues or Pentatonic — can be played in at least two ways (and often many more) on the harmonica, by using octave notes.

Riffs and Octave Scales

You can use the High Blues Scale to play Blues riffs — try this high version of the "Hoochie Talk" riff:

8 9̇ 8 9 ⑨̇   •   •   ★

Two Octave Blues Scale Riff

Try combining the two scales to create longer riffs — here's a simplified and a "regular" version (the regular one uses an extra 1 in to connect a down part and an up part):

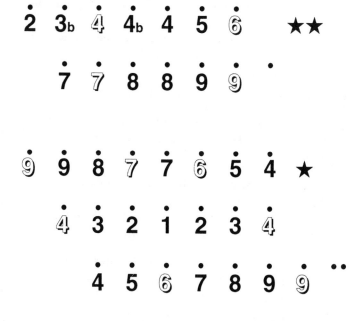

Make sure you know how to create riffs from the high octave Blues Scale, and how to combine different octave Blues Scales to create longer riffs, as in the examples above. Sometimes adding or leaving out a note makes a two octave Blues Scale riff work better...

Positions: A Real Definition!

Think about this. We just played eight *First Position* Major Scales in the last section. What did every single one of them have in common? They all began and ended on the same octave notes — the octave notes 1 out, 4 out, 7 out, and 10 out.

What did our four *Fourth Position* Minor Scales have in common? The same thing — they all began and ended on same octave notes — 6 in and 10 in.

And what did our three *Second Position* (simplified) Blues Scales have in common? They all began and ended on the same octave notes — 2 in, 6 out, and 9 out.

> **Important:** All of the scales in any one particular position always begin and end on the same octave notes. Read about the examples, above, if you don't understand this!

Three more facts:

• **We can play any of these scales on *any key* harmonica,** using the same tablature notation. This tablature notation tells us which holes to use, and whether to breathe in or out. It does not use note letter names at all.

• **The first note** (which is always the same as the last note) **of a scale gives that scale its name.** This is true for both note letter names (like B, or E flat) and for tablature names (like 2 in, or 4 out).

• Since the **note letter names change** whenever we use a different "key" harmonica, it is easier to describe scales on the harmonica by **tablature names** than by note letter names.

> So we can say that a position tells us (by tablature name, not note letter name) what hole (including all octave notes) a scale begins and ends on.
>
> If a scale begins and ends on the octave notes 1 out, 4 out, 7 out, or 10 out — that scale **has** to be in the First Position!
>
> Or we could say it like this: Whenever we are talking about **First Position,** we are talking about playing music using a scale that begins and ends on the octave notes 1 out, 4 out, 7 out, and 10 out.
>
> Whenever we are talking about **Second Position,** we are talking about playing music using a scale that begins and ends on the octave notes 2 in, 6 out, and 9 out.
>
> Whenever we are talking about **Fourth Position,** we are talking about playing music using a scale that begins and ends on the octave notes 6 in and 10 in (or, for benders, on 3 in bb also).

Same Position, New Scale

So far, we have only played one type of scale (Major, Minor, and Blues) in each position (First, Fourth, and Second). Some scales are certainly easier to play in certain positions than they are to play in other positions.

But it's easy to play two or more scales in a single position (even if we can't bend yet). Here's a new scale that begins and ends on the octave notes 2 in, 6 out, and 9 out. It's in the Second Position, but it's not a Blues Scale...

The Second Position "Country" Scale ★

Here is the easiest Country or Pentatonic Scale on the harmonica. It can be called the **"High End Second Position Pentatonic Scale:"**

⑥ **6 7 8** ⑧ ⑨

Here's a "Simplified Low End Second Position Pentatonic Scale" (it leaves out one bent note, the 3 in bb):

2 x 3 4 ⑤ ⑥

Country, R & B, and Blues Riffs ★

The Pentatonic Scale is often used in rock music, and sometimes in Blues, but it is especially important in creating improvisations for country or **C & W** music. As with any other scale, we choose scale notes and add some rhythm to form riffs from it. Here are a few easy ones.

⑥ **6 7 8** ⑧ ⑨ • • •

⑨ ⑧ **8 7** ⑥ ⑥ • • •

C & W riffs often use the top third of a lower octave scale, then one whole scale. Here's an example from my book *Country & Western Harmonica Made Easy* (page 93):

4 ⑤ ⑥ **7 8** ⑧ ⑨ ••• ••••

⑨ ⑧ **8 7** ⑥ ⑥ ⑤ ⑥ ••• ••••

Here's an R & B style usage of the Second Position Pentatonic Scale. The timing is a bit tricky, so I give you a "more dot" version, below. But the notes are easy (if you've learned the scale).

⑥ • **6 7 8** ⑧ ⑨ • • •

⑥ • • **6 7 8** ⑧ ⑨ ••• ••••

This scale is sometimes used in Blues music, as well. For example, Little Walter's song *"Juke"* takes the Simplified Second Position Pentatonic Scale, adds some rhythm, and uses it as a riff. Here is something similar:

2   **3**   **4**   5̲   6̲   6̲

More than one scale can begin and end on the same octave note. In other words, you can play more than one scale with one position. And if you like **C & W**, you'd better play this scale and these riffs, too.

Positions: Old-Fashioned View

We now know what positions are, and why they work. But where did they come from? Perhaps the pioneer African-American Blues harmonica players wanted a simple way to describe the two main styles of playing the harmonica. Or maybe the European style of players wanted to separate *their* style of playing from that of the upstart Blues harp players.

No one knows who first came up with the idea of positions. But long before World War Two it was clear that there were two main, but very different, styles of playing this simple and popular instrument: "Straight" Harp, and "Cross" Harp.

"Straight" Harp

"Straight" harp became the term used for players who played using the Major and Minor Scales built into the harmonica. If they had a key of C harmonica, they played their music in either C Major or A Minor. And no matter what key their harmonicas were in, they played most of their Major Songs using the 4 to 7 scale, and their Minor songs using the 6 to 10 scale.

They played classical music, and the folk music of Europe and Appalachia. If, occasionally, they played Blues — or tried to — it tended to have a very bouncy and brassy feel, rather than a Bluesy feel. But for most players, the term "Straight Harp Blues" would seem to be a contradiction — "Straight" and "Blues" just don't go together...

"Cross" Harp

"Cross" harp became a term used for Blues players who were using that (pretty) easy Blues Scale found between holes 2 in and 6 out to play Blues. Maybe they'd work their way down to the 1 in. But hardly ever go higher than the 6 hole.

And if someone suggested that they play a Blues in another position, well, "everybody plays Blues in cross harp." If they had a key of C harmonica, they would be playing Blues in the key of G, since their Blues Scale started on the 2 in note, a G.

First and Second "Positions"

As I mentioned, I've never been able to find out when the word "Position" first came into use. But at some point, the terms "First Position" also began to be used as a synonym for "Straight Harp." The term "Second Position" began to be used as a synonym for "Cross Harp."

These terms were not really accurate — after all, the Straight Harp players were using a completely different scale (in what we now call Fourth Position) to play their Minor Scale songs. But since no one was terribly interested in the music theory that underlay these terms, they caught on.

Position Myths

Of course, lots of players love to play in *both* the above styles. And perhaps I'm exaggerating the above views of straight versus cross harp. But in my 20 plus years of teaching harmonica, I've run into an awful lot of players who believe the two main myths about positions. One of these myths, especially, limits the playing of many Blues and rock harp musicians.

Myth Number One: "Straight" Harp

Many players believe that songs based in the Major Scale (which includes most folk and classical songs) can *only* be played in First, or Straight Position.

This part of the myth has quite a bit of truth to it. First Position is certainly the easiest way to play Major Scale songs. It also allows us to use lots of chords (notes played together) along with our single notes. But there are two good reasons to break this myth.

- The first is that players who can bend well are able to play Major Scales in other positions. Some of these are easier, some harder, some too hard to bother with (for me).

- The second and more important is that playing Major Scale songs in "Bluesier" positions is a wonderful way to play Blues versions of popular and folk songs. It allows us to combine the Major Scale with some Blues Scale notes — that's what makes the song sound "Bluesier." Even non-benders can learn to do this some, if they understand positions!

The flip side of Myth Number One is that Blues can't, or can't *really*, be played in First or Straight Position. But if you can bend notes, you can play great First Position Blues, as Jimmy Reed, Little Walter, Big Walter, Charlie Musselwhite, Magic Dick, and so many other great players demonstrate.

How do you do this? By playing the notes of the Blues Scale — in First Position! Your Blues Scale starts on the octave notes 1 out, 4 out, 7 out, or 10 out.

Myth Number Two: "Cross" Harp

Many players also believe that Blues riffs or songs can only be played in Second, or Cross Position.

It's true that Second Position is an easy key to play Blues in, with lots of chord possibilities and (relatively) easy bends. But there are at least four other positions that are no harder. And each of those four other positions has a fabulously different sound from Cross harp — almost like playing another instrument! Plus, for good benders, there are seven other, more difficult positions available.

Part One, Last Licks

You now have a pretty complete knowledge of what positions are, and why they work.

You also know how to use scales to create songs and riffs (although of course there's lots more to know about this, which is why I plan to write a book or three about it, before too long).

It's time to go on to Part Two. You'll learn how to play all the Blues Scales, and some of the other scales, in a variety of positions. And you'll leave far behind any "position myths" that you may have once held...

I'll begin Part Two by describing the most popular way of playing Blues music — a way that is also used in lots of rock and jazz. It's called the Twelve Bar Blues Structure, and if you don't already understand it, you're in for a treat! You can play "Twelve Bars" in any position — and you soon will!

Then I'll review advanced bending notation, and we'll be ready to get to the actual positions, starting with Second. We'll learn how to play Twelve Bars, Blues Scales, and riffs and solos in Second Position. Then we'll apply the same information to learn how to play them in First through Twelfth Positions.

About the Song Examples

Many of the partial song examples in both Part One and Part Two are included (in full length versions) in *The Pocket Harmonica Songbook.* For a listing of some of these songs and their positions see page 94.

PART TWO

Chord Structures

Just as notes that sound good together form chords, chords that sound good together are combined to form **chord structures.** A chord structure is simply two or more chords that are played in a certain order, with each chord played for a certain amount of time.

Skeletons and Flesh

A chord structure is a bit like a skeleton. Muscle, fat, hair, and skin "flesh out" a skeleton into a complete person. But the skeleton provides the basic structure.

A chord structure provides the basic underlying structure of a piece of music. Notes chosen from the Blues Scales (in the form of riffs and solos) "flesh out" this skeleton of the music into a complete song.

Playing a simple Twelve Bar Blues Structure won't produce exciting music. But it's a very important step towards being able to "flesh out" the skeleton of the Blues Chord Structure with great riffs and improvisations!

There are many different types of chord structures. Some types of music (like Blues) mostly use just one main chord structure. Other types of music, like country and western, or rock, mostly use a small number of different chord structures. And pop and jazz styles music use many different chord structures.

Unfortunately, this book won't cover many chord structures. In fact, we'll stick to the one most popular for Blues and rock music: **The Twelve Bar Blues.** So if you are interested in learning some of the other most important ones, for rock, jazz, pop, folk, and country — I recommend *Music Theory Made Easy.*

The Twelve Bar Blues

The **Twelve Bar Chord Structure** may be the most widely played chord structure in the whole world. Also called **"The Twelve Bar Blues,"** it is the underlying chord structure used for almost all Blues, a lot of rock, and quite a bit of jazz and country music. Turn to page 46 and play it now, if you like.

It's so important (especially if you plan to play with other musicians) that I'd like you to break down and read this entire section, not just the box!

What is a "Bar?"

The term **"bar"** simply refers to four beats of time. So one "verse" of a Twelve Bar Blues is 48 beats (or 4 beats X 12 bars) long. A Blues song is usually made up of anywhere from three or four verses on up.

Three Chords to the Blues

The Twelve Bar Blues Chord Structure usually uses just **three chords.** These three chords will always have the same relationship to each other, which we can describe using the Roman Numerals I, IV, and V. These three chords can be either Major chords, Minor chords, or Seventh chords.

A Blues that uses **Minor** chords will usually have a **slow, sad, feel.**

A Blues that uses **Major** chords will usually have a **faster, more upbeat feel.**

A Blues that uses **Seventh** chords can be **either slow** or **fast, sad** or **happy** — but it's sure to sound Bluesy!

Letter Names for the Blues Chords

Each of the three chords in a Blues can be called by three different names. One of these names is the "Letter Name" that we are already familiar with. This tells us what *specific* chord, like A Seventh, or C Major, to use — the letter names tell us what note the chord is based on.

Roman Numeral Names for Blues Chords

We can also use **Roman Numeral** names for chords. This gives us an easy way to refer to the three chords that make up a Blues chord structure, even if we have not decided on the specific chords (letter names) that we want to use.

Roman Numeral names are a really important and useful part of music theory, and every musician should eventually learn about them. But understanding Roman Numeral notation is a bit complicated. So if the following information is hard for you to understand, I take a bit more time and make it much easier in *Music Theory Made Easy*, page 94.

Roman Numeral names tell us about the **relationship** between notes (or the chords that are based on those notes). In Roman Numeral notation, each note of the Major Scale is given a Roman Numeral name.

DO	RE	MI	FA	SO	LA	TI	DO
I	II	III	IV	V	VI	VII	I

So the Roman Numeral "V" always refers to the fifth note of a Major Scale, no matter what key that scale is in. The "I" always refers to the first note, and so on.

The Roman Numeral names of the three chords of a Blues are the **I chord, the IV chord,** and **the V chord** (pronounced "one chord," "four chord," and "five chord."

Once we decide what key Blues music we are going to play, we automatically know what the three chords we need to use will be. We will use a chord based on the first note of that key's Major Scale, a chord based on the fourth note of that key's Major Scale, and a chord based on the fifth note of that key's Major Scale.

Charting the Blues

Here is a chart that tells you which chord to use, and how long to hold it for. I also include the chord letter names you'd use if you were playing this Blues in the key of G.

And lastly, I'll throw in one other (oh, no!) set of names for these chords, in Latin. Many musicians use these three names — **Tonic Chord, Subdominant Chord,** and **Dominant Chord** — so they are worth learning. Since these names are so long, just in the chart I'll put them in parentheses and abbreviate them as Tonic, Sub, and Dom.

The Twelve Bar Blues In the Key of G

Chord Letter Name	How Many Beats	How Many Bars	Roman & (Latin) Names
G	16	4	I (Tonic)
C	8	2	IV (Sub)
G	8	2	I (Tonic)
D	4	1	V (Dom)
C	4	1	IV (Sub)
G	8*	2*	I* (Tonic)
Totals:	48	12	*includes turnaround

> **Important:** You really need to learn the **Roman Numeral names (I - IV - V)** and the Latin Names for the parts of the Twelve Bar Blues:
>
> ## Tonic - Subdominant - Dominant
>
> You will also need to learn to hear (in your "gut" as well as your head) how long each chord lasts for, and exactly when one chord changes to the next.

What's A Turnaround?

Many Twelve Bar Blues end each verse with what is called a **"turnaround"**. A turnaround is just a **small chunk of V** (or Dominant) **chord** (from two to four beats worth) at the end of a verse that lets you know that one verse is ending, and another is about to begin. Using a turnaround is generally considered classier than shouting "Hey — This verse is over!" Some Blues verses don't have turnarounds at all. They just end with eight beats of tonic chord, and it's a little harder to hear when they end.

What's an Introduction?

Sometimes a Twelve Bar Blues song does not begin with a regular Twelve Bar Blues verse. Instead, it starts with one short chord structure (either eight or sixteen beats long) called an **introduction.** This introduction is then followed by a series of regular Twelve Bar Blues verses, until the end of the song. Not knowing about introductions has messed up many a harpist trying to play with a band, even if he or she knew the Twelve Bar Blues!

There are two main types of introduction. One is eight beats long, and looks just like the last line of my Twelve Bar Blues chart, including the turnaround. In a key of G Blues, it would look like this:

	Beats	Bars	
G	8*	2*	I* (Tonic)

*includes turnaround

The other is sixteen beats long, and looks just like the last three lines of my chart, including the turnaround.

	Beats	Bars	
D	4	1	V (Dom)
C	4	1	IV (Sub)
G	8*	2*	I* (Tonic)
Totals:	16	4	*includes turnaround

Second Position Twelve Bar Blues ★

Here's a very, very, simple **Second Position Twelve Bar Blues,** below. To liven it up, I have used both chords and single notes. Of course, in most positions, chords would not be available.

My chords are indicated by putting three numbers together, and underlining them. So for the first three beats of this Twelve Bar, play the notes 1 in - 2 in - 3 in at the same time.

Play all six lines (on this and the next page), then play it again, without stopping. Feel free to spice it up with any hand wahwahs or tongue rhythms (if you don't know how to do that, see one of my beginner's methods). Keep a nice steady beat! Tap that foot!

For your convenience, I have included the chords that a guitar player would use to accompany you if you were playing with a key of C harmonica (in little letters below the tablature). In Second Position, that means a Twelve Bar Blues in G. I've also included Roman Numerals I, IV, and V to help you remember the chords of the Blues.

I **123** 2 2 2
G

123 6 6 6
G

IV **345** 4 4 4
C

I **123** 2 2 2
G

Continued on next page!

Continued from previous page!

V **456** •   IV **4** **4** **4** •
   D   C

I **123** •   **Turn-** **4** **4** **4** •
   G   **around**
                D

To save space, I could notate the same simple **Twelve Bar Blues in G** like this:

2 **2** **2** **2**   **4** **4**
G   C

2 **2**   **4** **4**   **2** **4** •
G   D   C   G   D

The notation tells you which notes to use for each part of a Twelve Bar, and then you have to add articulations, hand wah wahs, or any other effects to liven it up. This shorter notation version is what I will use for the rest of this book, for the Twelve Bar Blues in different positions.

> Of course, most Twelve Bar Blues will use a far greater variety of "fleshing out" notes, chosen from one (or more) Blues Scales. But even this simple one above will help you to get the Twelve Bar feeling: If this chord structure is new to you, play it until you can hear exactly when the chords change from one to the other — in your sleep.

Improvising Hints

This is not a book on improvisation (although I am working on one). So if you don't already know how to improvise Blues and Rock music, you might want to check out my *Instant Blues Harmonica* series (Volumes One and Two), my *Three Minutes to™ Blues Harmonica* video, and or my *Music Theory Made Easy*. But here are a few hints on how to create your own Blues music.

Blues Scale Riffs in the Twelve Bars

It is very important to be able to play Twelve Bar Chord Structures by ourselves. But sometimes other musicians will provide a Twelve Bar Blues structure as "background music" for us to play solos with. When this happens, we don't need to worry quite so much about the structure (the other musicians will maintain it).

We can just play Blues Scale riffs that fit in with the background that the other musicians are providing. The easiest way to do this is to use the Blues Scale in the same key as our Twelve Bar Blues. If everyone is playing a Blues in D, we would just play riffs chosen from the notes of a D Blues Scale.

For example, we might fill up one Twelve Bar Solo verse (48 beats long) with six of the eight beat Blues Scale Riffs from page 33 (6 times 8 = 48). As long as we use the correct key harp (see Parts Two and Three, for that), riffs or solos created from the Blues Scale *have got to sound great* when played against a Blues "background" in the same key as that Blues Scale. Grab your guitarist, and wail!

And instead of playing composed riffs — riffs that have already been written down — we can also choose combinations of notes from the Blues Scale, and create our own.

Choose two or three or four notes from the Second Position Blues Scale, and practice putting them together to form riffs. You'll probably find that beginning and ending a riff on a 2 in or 6 out will sound best, at first.

Study the rhythm patterns used by the riffs of page 33, but substitute your own chosen notes. Or try using the same notes as I did, but vary the rhythm patterns. That's all I did on page 33 — took the notes of the Blues Scale, and applied various eight beat rhythm patterns to them!

Multiple Position Blues Scale Blues

Here's an amazing little fact that gives us a great way to create interesting sounding Twelve Bar Blues.

In some positions, you can easily use additional Blues Scales **from other positions** during the Subdominant (or "IV") and Dominant (or "V") parts of a Twelve Bar Blues. For example, when playing in Second Position we can (of course) use notes from the Second Position Blues Scale during the Tonic or "I" parts. But instead of using that same Blues Scale during the Subdominant, we'll use notes from the First Position Blues Scale! And notes from the Third Position Blues Scale during our Dominant ant and Turnaround parts!

I'll go into more detail on this when I describe each position in detail. It's easier than it sounds, when you try some simple examples!

> As you study the scales, solos, and riffs in each position that follows, there are two things that will help you to improvise. The first is to re-read the sections on creating riffs and solos from scales in Part One. The second is to learn how to use the "Multiple Position" Blues Scales improvisation strategy discussed just above.
>
> If you do these two things, you can create your own riffs from the scales in various positions, and put them together to form solos! That's "all" there is to it, but it takes a lifetime of experimenting and practice!

That's It for Music Theory

You now know more music theory that I did for the first ten or fifteen years of my playing career. And probably more theory than 95% of all amateur harp players! Congratulations!

More Bending Notation

Sorry, but this is not a book on how to bend. So if you want to use the advanced bending techniques discussed in this section (and used in some of the material in the rest of the book) — you know what to do (page 94).

But whether you can play the bends or not, it's worth learning how to read them in notation, so you can see when and where they are used.

Bending Notation Review

• A single "b" indicates a bent note that is bent down one half step (page 10), that is, just slightly. This is as far as 1 in, 4 in, and 6 in can be bent. 5 in can be bent almost to this depth, but not quite.

• A double "bb" indicates notes that are bent down two half steps. This sign will be seen most often on the 2 in and 3 in and 10 out bent notes. It is as far as the 2 in and 10 out notes can be bent.

• A triple "bbb" indicates notes that are bent down three half steps. Only one triple "bbb" is possible on the harmonica: a totally bent 3 in note.

For Expert Benders Only

I use small "#" symbols, or "sharp" signs, to indicate overblow and overdraw notes. These are the hardest bends, and rarely used. The overblows are found on the mid-range out notes, and the overdraws in the high end.

• The notes 4 out and 6 out can be overblown **up** (yes up, not down) three half steps, as shown by the notations 4### and 6###. The notes 8 in and 9 in can (by some) be overdrawn up by three half steps, too.

• The note 5 out can be overblown up by two half steps, as shown by 5##. The note 7 in can be over-drawn by two half steps, too, as shown by 7##.

Bending Notation Examples

Saints and *Twinkle* are in First Position, *F & J* in Ninth!

Oh	when	the	saints	go	mar-	chin'	in
1	2	2bb	2	1	2	2bb	2

Fran-	kie	and	John-	nie	were	sweet-	hearts
3bbb	4	4###	5	4###	4	3bbb	3bbb

Twin-	kle	twin-	kle	lit-	tle	star
1	1	2	2	3bb	3bb	2

Please read this entire section if you want to understand my notation system for advanced bending.

The Positions

> The rest of this book is divided into one section for each of the twelve positions. Each section features Twelve Bar Blues, Blues Scales, and other scales, plus hints and tips for every level of player.

The more commonly useful positions, especially First, Second, Third, Fourth, and Fifth Positions, will be covered in more detail. But I'll include sections on all of them, for those of you who like challenges (actually, some riffs in strange positions are easy, so watch the stars).

> I choose to start with Second Position, since it's the most commonly used for Blues. And all of the material that we cover for Second Position will be repeated for the other, less familiar (and often more technically difficult) positions. I'll describe each part of the Second Position Section (like *Twelve Bars*, *Good Note Combinations*, etc.), and these descriptions will apply to all of the other positions, too.

Start with the section on Second Position, and make sure that you can play a simple Twelve Bar Blues, and (at least) the Simplified Blues Scales. These will be old friends, from Part One.

Then you will be ready to start playing the Twelve Bar Blues and Scales and other material in the other positions. Work with First and Third Positions until you can play their Twelve Bars and Scales, then go on to Fourth, Fifth, and the rest.

> You may want to go to page 86 and check out the PositionFinder™ before you've learned all of the positions — nothing wrong with that!

The Position Charts

The chart just beneath the heading for each position tells you which key harmonica you need to use with which key music, in that position. You can use this chart in two ways. We'll use Second Position as an example.

Know Music Key, Want Harp Key

If you know the **key of the music** that you want to play:

• Find it in the *bottom* line. Let's say that you want to play a Twelve Bar Blues in "Bb," for example.

• Then look directly on top of the Bb in the Music Key (bottom) line, and you'll see that Eb appears in the **top (Harp Key) line.** So in Second Position, if you want to play a Twelve Bar Blues in Bb, you will need an Eb harmonica.

Harp Key: C Db D <u>Eb</u> E F Gb G Ab A Bb B
Music Key: G Ab A <u>Bb</u> B C Db D Eb E F Gb

Have Harp Key, Need Music Key

If, instead, you know the **key of the harmonica** that you want to use:

- Look it up in the *top* line. A G harp, for example.

- Then look directly below the G in the Harp Key (top) line, and you'll see that D appears in the bottom line. So in Second Position, if you want to use a G harp, you will be playing your Twelve Bar Blues in the key of D.

Harp Key: C Db D Eb E F Gb <u>G</u> Ab A Bb B
Music Key: G Ab A Bb B C Db <u>D</u> Eb E F Gb

Counting Half Steps

I also include another way to figure out which harp to use with which key music. If you have memorized all of the notes of the keyboard, you can count half steps.

For example, in Second Position, the harp key is always 5 half steps above the music key. If your music is in the key of G, just think of all the keyboard note names. Start on the G, but *do not* count it. Count half steps until you get to the fifth one, which is C: (G) Ab A Bb B C.

A Bb B C Db D Eb E F Gb G Ab (jump back to A)

> **Caution:** Never confuse the **harp key** with the **music key**! To use this method, you must start with the music key, and count up to the harp key. If you want to start with the harp key, you must count **down** five half steps to get the music key!

Count Up Four for Cross Harp? Wrong!

In the past, harp players have said that "Second Position harmonica is four notes above the music." This works for harmonicas in the keys of G, A, C, D, and F (since G to C is four notes, and so on). But try figuring it out this way for the other keys (which require sharp # and flat b notes), and you'll be confused, or wrong, or both!

The "Feel" of the Position

Because certain notes of the scales are easier or harder to get in different positions, each position tends to produce a different "feel" when playing Blues or rock music. Of course, if you're a top bender, you can play any notes you like. But even intermediate players will tend to find that Third Position produces easy to play Blues with a sad feel, and First Position (especially in the high end) produces easy to play Blues in a happy, boisterous mood.

Make sure that you understand how to use the chart at the beginning of each position section. It tells you which key harmonica to play with what key music, for that position, and the "feel" of the position.

Second Position

Second position is traditionally the most popular Blues position. You can call this Blues Scale a "Myxolydian-based (Mix - oh - **lid** - ee - in) Blues Scale" if you want to impress your jamming partners (Myxolydian is an old-fashioned term that refers to an older scale that has some similarities to the Second Position). I've already given you lots of info about this position, so let's keep moving!

Harp key is always 5 half steps above the music key.

Harp Key: C Db D Eb E F Gb G Ab A Bb B
Music Key: G Ab A Bb B C Db D Eb E F Gb

"Feel" of Position: Bluesy! Could be happy or sad, depending on whether you play it faster or slower, and what notes you emphasize. This makes it the most versatile of all the positions.

Second Position Twelve Bar ★

Here's a very simple **Second Position Twelve Bar Blues,** below. The guitar chords written under each line will work when used with a harmonica in the key of C. (I also use a key of C harp as an example for all the other position Twelve Bars. If you want to use a different key harp, use the key charts to tell your guitarist what key to play in.)

I may also include a "nicer" or more interesting Twelve Bar, so that you can get a feel for that position's Blues. In these "nicer" Twelve Bars, you will notice that I usually use Blues Scale Riffs based on the Simplified Blues Scale notes for the "Tonic" parts. I may also use the "Multiple Position Blues Scale Blues Riffs" (first mentioned on page 48) for the "Subdominant" and "Dominant" parts, as I do at the end of this section.

Twelve Bar Octave Substitutions

In this section I will give you the other octave notes that you can substitute for the parts of the Twelve Bar Blues. For example, instead of just using 2 in for all your "I" or "Tonic" parts (the "G" sections in my above example), you could use 6 out or 9 out. Same for the other parts.

On the following page you'll find the Second Position Octave Notes, with a sample Twelve Bar using them. In the rest of the positions, you'll have to make up your own Octave Substituting Twelve Bar — it's easy! Just use any Tonic (I) notes for the Tonic parts, any Subdominant (IV) notes for the Subdominant parts, and any Dominant (V) notes for the Dominant and turnaround parts!

Tonic (I): 2 = ③ = ⑥ = ⑨

Subdominant (IV): ④ = ① = ⑦ = ①⓪

Dominant (V): 4 = 1 = 8

Octave Substitution Twelve Bar: ★

It looks different than the 2 in - 4 out - 4 in version, but sounds very similar. Make up variations of your own.

••••	••••	••••	••••		••••	••••
2	⑥	⑨	**2**		①	①⓪
G					C	

••••	••••		••••	••••		••••	•••	•
2	⑥		①	①		⑥	④	
G			D	C		G	D	

Easy Improv Strategy

If there is a safe and easy way to improvise in a position, I'll give it to you here. For example, in Second Position, use **any in notes from 1 in to 5 in.** They will always sound at least okay.

Simplified "Blues Scale" ★

Whenever possible, I will give you a partial or approximate "Blues Scale" that you can play without bending. It won't be as good as the real thing, but it will work. Here is a no bend "Blues Scale" for Second Position. You can use it along with the Part One instructions for creating riffs out of scales on pages 30 - 33 and 47 - 48.

		dwah		dwah		
2	**3**	④	**4**	**4**	**5**	⑥

⑥	**7**	⑦	**8**	**8**	**9**	⑨

Easiest Blues Scale ★★

This is the easiest Blues Scale available in this position. Yup, it requires bending — they all do. Use it with the Part One instructions on creating riffs out of scales.

2 3b ④ 4b 4 5 ⑥

Easy Note Combinations ★

Choosing a couple of notes from the Simplified Blues Scale often gives us convenient and easy to use note combinations. In this section I'll give you some "safe" notes combos to use, plus a riff or three created from them as examples. This will be even more important in the harder positions, where there are not as many easy things to play as in Second Position.

We use these Easy Note Combos to create riffs, simply by adding a bit of rhythm. But of course you can choose *any* three or two or four notes from the scales (they don't even have to be next to each other), and use them to make up riffs. Check out these examples, below (which of course include "*Hoochie Talk*"). The Easy Note Combos are in the first line, then the riffs created from them.

	dwah					
2	3	4	4		4	5	6

	dwah		dwah		dwah		dwah	
2	3	4	4	4	3	2	2

	dwah		dwah	
2	3	4	3	4

4 5 4 5 6

> **HINT: For timing help with riffs,** play the ones on page 74 — they're easy and clear timing-wise! Also, try the first two riffs above as four beaters, tapping on the **big dots** only. Often you'll need to experiment with the beat in this way, to make some riffs fit into a Twelve Bar — be flexible with timing!

Other Blues Scales

If other Blues Scales can be played in the position, I'll provide them here. Often these other Blues Scales are played using different octaves. For example, this next one starts out like the last one, then jumps down an octave to the 1 out, and works its way back up.

2   3b   1   1b   1   2bb   2   ★★

The next "other Blues Scale" is in the higher octave. It requires an overblow and the tricky 7 overdraw, so it's a four star production. ★★★★

6   6###   7   7##   8   9   9

Here's one more "other" Blues Scale in Second Position.

9   10bb   10   1b   1   2bb   2 ★★

Three Octave Blues Scale ★★★★

If a long riff made of more than one Blues Scale is not too hard, I'll put it here. Add any rhythm you like to this one!

9   10bb1   1b   1   2bb   2

3b   4   4b   4   5   6

6###   7   7##   8   9   9

The Second Position Major Scales

If one or more Major Scales can be played (reasonably easily) in the position, I'll provide them here. They will be presented in order of difficulty.

6 6 7 7 8 8 9b 9 ★★

2 3bb 3 1 1 2 2b 2 ★★

2 3bb 3 4 4 5 5## 6 ★★★

To use these scales, practice one, then take a Major Scale Song that you know well, and try to play it using the scale you've learned. Here's are two examples:

Oh	when	the	saints	go	mar-	chin'	in
6	7	7	8	6	7	7	8

Oh	when	the	saints	go	mar-	chin'	in
2	3	4	4	2	3	4	4

Bluesy Melodies in Second Position ★★

By taking a song that you usually play in First Position, and playing it in Second, you can add Blues licks for a "Bluesy" feeling. Why bother? Because it's much "Bluesier" than the usual First Position version, and lets you throw in great Blues riffs!

First learn the Second Position Blues Scale and at least one of the Second Position Major Scales. Learn the first line or two of your song using the Second Position Major Scale (with any luck you won't even need to use the hard bends). Lots of these in my *Pocket Harmonica Songbook!*

On notes of the song that are held for a long time (like the word "saints," throw in a short lick from the Second Position Blues Scale, like I do. And try playing it with half as many taps, once you've got the feel of it.

Oh	when	the	saints	•	•	•	•
2	3	4	4	2	2bb	1	2

Go	mar-	chin'	in	•	•	•	•
2	3	4	4	6	5	4	2

The Second Position Minor Scale

If one or more Minor Scales can be played (reasonably easily) in the position, I'll provide them here. They will be presented in order of difficulty.

6 6 6### 7 8 8b 9 9 ★★

2 3bb 3b 4 4 4### 5 6 ★★★

To use these new Minor Scales, practice them, then take a Minor Scale Song that you know well, and try to play it. Here's an example:

A-	las	my	lo-	ve	you	do	me	wrong
⑥	⑥###	⑦	8	⑧b	8	7	6	5

Multiple Position Blues Scale Blues ★★

When playing Second Position Blues, we can use notes chosen from the Second Position Blues Scales to create our Second Position Twelve Bars.

Or, if we're a bit more musically adventurous, we can use notes from the First Position Blues Scales during our "Subdominant" parts, and notes from the Third Position Blues Scale during out "Dominant" (and "turnaround") parts. This works due to the way that the parts of the Twelve Bar Blues, and the positions, are related to each other musically (see page 76).

Note: And they are incredibly related! The last three notes of one position may be the first three of another — look at First and Second Positions, for an example!

Here's an example of this type of Second Position Twelve Bar. You can hear how "right" it sounds. You might want to check out the First and Third Position Blues Scales that follow, to see how I've used them in this example.

IMPORTANT: Notice that the first line is **repeated,** to form the 16 beats of the first Tonic part.

2 3b 4 4b 4 5 ⑥ (repeat it!)
G — Tonic: Second Position Blues Scale

1 2 2bb 2b 2 3b 4
C — Subdominant: First Position Blues Scale

2 3b 4 4b 4 5 ⑥
G — Tonic:Second Position Blues Scale Again

4 5 ⑥ 6   1 2 2bb
D — Dominant: Third Pos. B. S.   C — Subdom:First Pos. B. S.

2 3b 4 4b   4 5 ⑥
G — Tonic: Second Pos. B. S.   D— Turnaround:Third Pos. B.S.

Something similar can be done in a number of different positions, especially First through Fifth. I'll tell you which other position Blues Scales you can use in the "Subdominant" and "Dominant" parts of each Twelve Bar in these positions. But be warned — in some positions this will be much harder to do than simply using the "main" or "Tonic" Blues Scale (review pages 47 - 48).

Creating Riffs from Blues Scales ★★

> If you learn a riff in one position, you will be able to "translate" it into other positions, by using notes from the Blues Scales of those other positions.

Muddy Waters used a riff similar to this one in his unforgettable song "*I'm A Man*," but it has also been used in settings as diverse as a hamburger commercial, the soundtrack for a Hollywood movie ("*Blue Collar*"), and a Beatles song, plus many more.

It is most often played in Second Position, and requires a bend on the 3 in. Start with simplified timing, then real.

2 4̊ 3b 2 ●●● ●●●●

2 4̊ 3b 2 ˙ ˙

Notice that it starts on the first note of the Second Position Blues Scale, then goes to the third note, the second note, and ends on the first note. Here's the same riff in First, Third, Fourth, Fifth, and Sixth Positions. Look up these other position Blues Scales to see how the same notes (first note, third note, second note, first note) of the Blues Scale are used to create the riff in each position!

7 9 8̊b 7 ˙ ˙ (First Pos.) ★★

4 6̊ 5 4 ˙ ˙ (Third Pos.) ★

6 8 7 6 ˙ ˙ (Fourth Pos.) ★

5̊ 6 6 5̊ ˙ ˙ (Fifth Pos.) ★

3 5̊ 4 3 ˙ ˙ (SixthPos.) ★

Multiple Position Riff Blues Example ★

Try using the above riffs to create a Multiple Position Twelve Bar Blues solo. To do it based in Second Position:

- Play the Second Position Riff four times. (For the Tonic-I)
- Play the First Position Riff twice. (Subdominant - IV)
- Repeat the Second Position Riff twice. (Tonic - I)
- Play the Third Position Riff once. (Dominant - V)
- Play the First Position Riff once. (Subdominant - IV)
- Play the Second Position Riff once. (Tonic - I)
- Play the Third Position Riff once. (Dominant/turn - V)

Use the Multiple Positions info in Third, Fourth, and Fifth Positions to create Twelve Bar solos from this above riff. In Third Position, you'd use 3rd - 2nd - 3rd- 4th - 2nd- 3rd - 4th riffs instead of the 2nd - 1st- 2nd - 3rd- 1st - 2nd - 3rd riffs used above.

First Position

First Position is the easiest way to play melodies that use the Major Scale — they just about play themselves! It's also great for Blues, especially if you can bend your high blow notes! For non-benders, I've given you an extra "nice but easy" Twelve Bar, to get the feel of this great but underused Blues position.

Harmonica is always in the same key as the music. So you don't need a chart. Music in the key of A, harp in the key of A, and so on!

"Feel" of Position: The easy availability of Major Scale notes tends to give a bouncy, upbeat, happy Blues feel, especially in the high end. Great for medium or fast "shuffle" or "boogie woogie" based Blues or Rock music.

First Position Twelve Bar ★

4	4	4	4		5	5
C					F	

4	4		2	5		4	2	•
C			G	F		C	G	

Twelve Bar Octave Substitutions

Make up your own First Position Octave Substitution Twelve Bar Blues by using some of these other octave notes in place of the Tonic 4 out, Subdominant 5 in, and Dominant 2 in (the same as the Second Position Tonic).

Tonic (I): $4 = 1 = 7 = 10$

Subdominant (IV): $5 = 9 = 2bb$

Dominant (V): $2 = 3 = 6 = 9$

Nicer First Position Twelve Bar ★

Notice that I use the Simplified First Position Rule (out only) to create the tonic parts of this Blues Twelve Bar.

4	5	6	5	4	5	6	(repeat)
C							

5	6	7	6	5	6	7
F						

4	5	6	5	4	5	6
C						

Continued on next page!

Continued from previous page.

$$\overset{\bullet}{2} \quad \overset{\bullet}{3} \quad \overset{\bullet}{4} \quad \overset{\bullet}{3} \qquad \overset{\bullet}{5} \quad \overset{\bullet}{6} \quad \overset{\bullet}{\overline{7}} \quad \overset{\bullet}{}$$

G   F

$$\overset{\bullet}{\underline{4}} \quad \overset{\bullet}{\underline{5}} \quad \overset{\bullet}{\underline{6}} \quad \overset{\bullet}{\underline{5}} \qquad \overset{\bullet}{\underline{4}} \quad \overset{\bullet}{3} \quad \overset{\bullet}{4} \quad \overset{\bullet}{}$$

C   G

Easy Improv Strategy ★

Blow out! That's the easiest thing to do in First Position, and it will always work. Use clear, single, high notes, even if you can't bend them — wet your lips, then slide 'em and "dwah" them.

Easy Note Combinations

dwah   dwah   dwah   dwah

7   8   9   10

Easiest Pentatonic Scale ★

Use these scales for Blues, rock, or country music if you can't bend yet. I've put some rhythm to these, but make up rhythms of your own, too.

$$\overset{\bullet}{\underline{4}} \quad \overset{\bullet}{4} \quad \overset{\bullet}{\underline{5}} \quad \overset{\bullet}{6} \quad \overset{\bullet}{6} \quad \overset{\bullet}{\overline{7}} \quad \cdots$$

$$\overset{\bullet}{\overline{7}} \quad \overset{\bullet}{6} \quad \overset{\bullet}{6} \quad \overset{\bullet}{\underline{5}} \quad \overset{\bullet}{4} \quad \overset{\bullet}{\underline{4}} \quad \cdots$$

$$\overset{\bullet}{\overline{7}} \quad \overset{\bullet}{8} \quad \overset{\bullet}{8} \quad \overset{\bullet}{9} \quad \overset{\bullet}{10}\overset{\bullet}{10} \quad \cdots$$

Blues Scales

There is no "bend-free" Blues Scale for First Position. In the first line, the second note should be a 2 out bend, but this is a virtually impossible note to get, so I substitute a 2 out. Since there are Blues Scales in all parts of the harmonica in this position, I'll let you put them together to make combined Blues Scales. Also, use them to make riffs, as I've demonstrated with Second Position in Part One (page 31). Play them going up, then down.

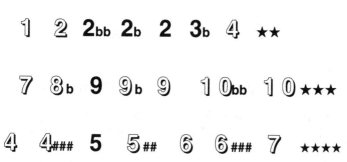

1   2   **2**bb **2**b **2** **3**b 4   ★★

7   8b   **9**   9b   9   10bb   10 ★★★

4   4### **5**   5##   6   6###   7   ★★★★

Fun Riff Ideas ★★★

Play a repeated riff using the low Blues Scale, adding in other riffs from the high one. Try it with *"Hoochie Talk"*:

2 **3**b **2** **3**b **4̇** **1̇0** **1̇0**bb

2 **3**b **2** **3**b **4̇** **10** **1̇0**bb **9** **10**

In the Style of Mr. Jimmy Reed

The immortal Jimmy Reed was a noted First Position Blues player (and one of my first harp influences). Perhaps half of his recorded songs areTwelve Bar Blues in First Position, with the rest in Second.

Mr. Reed used mostly high octave riffs in his First Position songs. His blow bends are clean and sharp, and even notes that are not actually bent are often begun with a slight bend (what I would call a "dwah" articulation).

Here's a 16 beat riff that I've tried to create in Mr. Reed's style. Hit the "dwahs" forcefully, and release them completely before moving smoothly to the next note.

dwah   dwah

8̇b **9** **8̇**b ᐧᐧ **1̇0** **1̇0**bb **9̇** **8** ᐧᐧᐧ

dwah   dwah   dwah

8̇b **9̇** **10** **9** **1̇0** **9** **10** **9̇** ᐧᐧ

Three Octave Blues Scale ★★★★

If a long riff made of more than one Blues Scale is not *too* hard, I'll put it here. This one's pretty darn hard!

1̇ **2̇** **2̇**bb **2̇**b **2** **3**b **4̇**

4̇### **5** **5̇**## **6̇** **6̇**### **7**

8̇b **9** **9̇**b **9** **1̇0**bb **1̇0** ᐧ

A Magic Dick Style First Position Ending

This riff, somewhat in the style of the great rock harpist Magic Dick, late of the J. Geils Band, takes the place of the last four bars (Dom - Subdom - Tonic and turnaround) of the last verse of a song (it only works for the last verse). It ends, basically, on a high Blues Scale with some rhythm and a few added notes. Magic Dick is still playing, so watch carefully for his gigs and catch a living rock legend!

Swing the rhythm, if you can. Notice the slightly difficult rhythm of lines two and three — if that seems too hard, just take your time hitting the last two notes.

3 **4** **3** **2** **4** **3b** **2** **2bb** **2**

Dominant   Subdominant

1 **1** **2** **2** **2bb** 2bb **2b** 2b

Tonic (no turnaround for last verse)

2 3b **3** **4** 1 0 **1** **0bb**

More Major Scales

4 **4** **5** **5** **6** **6** **7** **7** ★

1 **1** **2** **2bb** **2** **3bb** **3** **4** ★★

7 **8** **8** **9** **9** **10** **10b** **10**★★

Now work on some songs using these scales!

Oh	when	the	saints		go	mar-	chin'	in	
1	2	**2bb**	2		1	2	**2bb**	2	

Fran-	kie	and	John-	nie	were	sweet-	hearts	
1	2	**2**	**3bb**	**2**	2	1	1	

Twin-	kle	twin-	kle	lit-	tle	star
1	1	**2**	**2**	**3bb**	**3bb**	**2**

Oh	when	the	saints		go	mar-	chin'	in	
7	8	**9**	9		7	8	**9**	9	

Fran-	kie	and	John-	nie	were	sweet-	hearts	
7	8	9	**10**	9	8	7	7	

Multiple Position Blues Scale Blues

When playing First Position Blues, you can use (naturally) the First Position Blues Scales during your Tonic parts. You can also use Twelfth Position Blues Scales (good luck — they're hard!) during your Subdominants — but I don't suggest it, unless you're an advanced player. Instead, use lots of 5 in during the Subdominant, plus any other note that feels good! A more useful suggestion is that you can use your favorite Second Position Blues Scale riffs during your Dominant and Turnaround parts of a First Position Twelve Bar.

Third Position

In some ways, I think that Third Position is the easiest way to sound Bluesy for beginners. If you can get single notes, you can play a fine Blues Scale with just one (relatively) easy bent note, and use lots of slides and chords.

Third Position (as you may remember from my Minor Scale discussion, page 21) easily produces the Dorian Minor Scale, which you'll learn in a minute. You can call this Blues Scale a "Dorian-Based Blues Scale," if you want to impress other musicians.

Harp key is always 2 half steps below the music key.

Harp Key:	C	Db	D	Eb	E	F	Gb	G	Ab	A	Bb	B
Music Key:	D	Eb	E	F	Gb	G	Ab	A	Bb	B	C	Db

"Feel" of Position: The easy to get Dorian Minor notes tend to give a sad or plaintive feel, especially in the mid- or low range. Fast high end riffs can be happy sounding, in a slightly "eerie" or "wild" way.

Third Position Twelve Bar (C harp) ★

I'll also present a "nicer" Twelve Bar for Third Position later on, when I do the "Multiple Position Blues Scales Blues" below.

4 **4** **4** **4** **⑥** **⑥**
D   G

4 **4** **6** **⑥**   **4** **6** •
D   A   G   D   A

Twelve Bar Octave Substitutions

Make up your own Third Position Octave Substitution Twelve Bar Blues by using some of these other octave notes in place of the Tonic 4 in, Subdominant 6 out (same as the Tonic in Second Position), and Dominant 6 in.

Tonic (I): 4 = 1 = 8

Subdominant (IV): 2 = ③ = ⑥ = ⑨

Dominant (V): 6 = 10 = 3bb

Easy Improv Strategy ★

The Simplest Rule is still "use the in notes from 4 in to 10 in. If you want a rule that's the least bit harder, but will be more interesting, try this.

Memorize the following breathing pattern. Then try it while moving around *anywhere* on holes 4 to 10. It works because it mimics (more or less) the Third Position Blues Scale, as you'll see in a minute.

in out in out in out in

Easy Little Walter Style Riff ★

Combining the Simplest Rule with some sliding, and the new breathing pattern rule might give you a solo in the style of Little Walter, a wonderful Third Position player. The little numbers under the word "slide" indicate an in slide down then up, in between the beats.

dwah dwah   dwah dwah

8   8 slide 8   •   8   8 slide 8 •
        76567   76567

8 7 6 6 5 4   •••

Simplified "Blues Scales" ★

Here are two no bend "Blues Scales" for Third Position. As with any other Blues Scales, use them along with the Part One instructions for creating riffs out of scales.

             dwah

4 5 6 6 6 7 8

8 9 9 10 10 7 8

Easy Note Combinations ★

These note combinations from the Simplified Blues Scale can always be used to create good Third Position riffs, as the examples show. Notice the use of a Third Position *"Hoochie Talk"* riff, below!

4 5 6 6   6 7 8

6 7 6 7 8

    dwah
    6 6 5 4

6 7 6 7 8

    dwah
    5 6 5 6

6 7 6 7 8

Easiest Third Position Blues Scale ★★

Even if you can't bend much, "dwah" the first of the two
6 in notes and you'll have a pretty good Blues Scale.

4   5   6̃   6b   6   7̃   8

Other Blues Scales

The low end Third Position Blues Scale sounds great if
you start and end it with a "tongue blocked" 14 in chord
(mouth covers 1-2-3-4 holes, tongue covers 2 and 3 holes).
Notice the tricky 3 in bends.

1   2bb   2   3bbb   3bb   4̃   4   ★★★

The next "other Blues Scale" jumps from the high to the
middle octave.

8   9   9̃   6b   6   7̃   8   ★★

Tribute to Musselwhite ★ or ★★

Charlie Musselwhite, friend and Bluesman *Extraordinaire*,
often uses 1-4 octave blocks in low Third Position riffs.
See him in person when he tours in your area! The first
two line version is easy (except for the octave block,
described in the last section), the second one harder.

14̲⁞   1̲4̲⁞   14̲   25̲   14̲   •••

14̲   1̲4̲   6   6̃   5   4   •••

14̲⁞   1̲4̲⁞   14̲   25̲   14̲   •••

14̲   1̲4̲   3bbb   2   2bb   1   •••

Two Octave Blues Scale Solo

Combine the low and the middle octave Third Position
Blues Scales with a bit of rhythm for a great short solo (or
long riff):

8   7̃   6   6b   6̃   5   4

4̃   3bb   3bbb   2   2bb   1

The Third Position Minor Scale ★ or ★★

Practice these variations on the Minor Scale, called the **Dorian Minor Scale.** Then try playing *Saint James Infirmary, House of the Rising Sun,* or *Greensleeves.*

4	5	5	6	6	7	7	8

1	2	2bb	2	3bb	3	4	4

A-	las	my	lo-	ve	you	do	me	wrong
4	5	6	6	7	6	6	5	4

Well	I	went	down	to
4	5	6	6	5

	Saint	James	In-	firm-	ry
	6	6	6	5	4

There	is	a	house	in	New	Or-	leans
4	6	6	5	4	4	2	3b

Multiple Pos. Blues Scale Blues ★ or ★★

In Third Position, this improvising strategy works great! Use riffs chosen from the Third Position Blues Scale for your Tonic parts, riffs chosen from the Second Position Blues Scale for your Subdominant parts, and riffs chosen from the Fourth Position Blues Scale for your Dominant and Turnaround. Here's one that just uses the scales (or pieces of them, in the shorter parts). Can't bend? Dwah!

4	5	6	6b	6	7	8		(repeat)

D — Tonic: Third Position Blues Scale

2	3b	4	4b	4	5	6	

G — Subdominant: Second Position Blues Scale

4	5	6	6b	6	7	8	

D — Tonic: Third Position Blues Scale Again

6	7	8	8b		2	3b	4	

A — Dominant: Fourth Pos. B. S.   G — Sub: Second Pos.B.S.

4	5	6	6b		6	8	7

D — Tonic: Third Pos. B. S.   A — Turnaround:Fourth Pos. B. S.

Fourth Position

We've already used Fourth Position as the best way to play Minor Scale songs (although Third Position works pretty well, too). Now let's consider the use of Fourth Position for Blues and Rock improvisation, then cover a few Minor Scales that use bent notes.

Harp key is always 3 half steps above the music key.

Harp Key: C Db D Eb E F Gb G Ab A Bb B
Music Key: A Bb B C Db D Eb E F Gb G Ab

"Feel" of Position: The easy to get Minor Scale notes mix with the Blues Scale to make this good for sad or plaintive Blues. More often used in slow than fast songs. Definitely use for *anything* — Blues, Rock, or other — that uses **Minor Chords!**

Fourth Position Twelve Bar (C harp) ★

Fourth Position is especially useful for Blues Songs that use Minor Chords. These songs usually have a slow, sad, feel. Here's the easiest Fourth Position Twelve Bar Blues.

Twelve Bar Octave Substitutions

Make up your own Fourth Position Octave Substitution Twelve Bar Blues by using some of these other octave notes in place of the tonic 6 in, subdominant 4 in, and dominant 5 out.

Tonic (I): 6 = 10 = 3bb

Subdominant (IV): 4 = 1 = 8

Dominant (V): 2 = 5 = 8

Fancier Fourth Position Twelve Bar ★

On the next page is a slightly fancier Twelve Bar to help you get the feel of Fourth Position Blues. Play it slowly and sadly. Notice the use of "multiple" positions: the Fourth Position Blues Scale during the Tonic parts, the Third Position Blues Scale during the Subdominants, and parts of the Fifth Position Blues Scale during the Dominant and Turnaround.

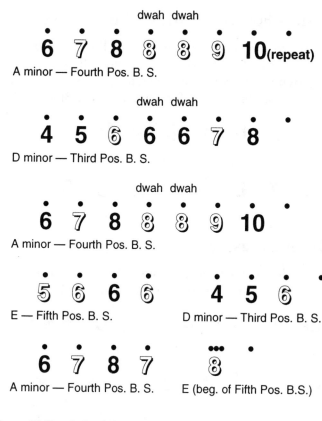

A minor — Fourth Pos. B. S.

D minor — Third Pos. B. S.

A minor — Fourth Pos. B. S.

E — Fifth Pos. B. S.

D minor — Third Pos. B. S.

A minor — Fourth Pos. B. S.

E (beg. of Fifth Pos. B.S.)

Simplified "Blues Scales" ★

There's no easy improv strategy for Fourth Position, other than using the Blues Scales and Easy Note Combos. Here are two no bend "Blues Scales." Dwah those blow notes!

Easy Note Combinations ★

These three combinations of notes from the Simplified Blues Scale will always create good Fourth Position riffs. Check out the Fourth Position "*Hoochie Talk*" riff, below!

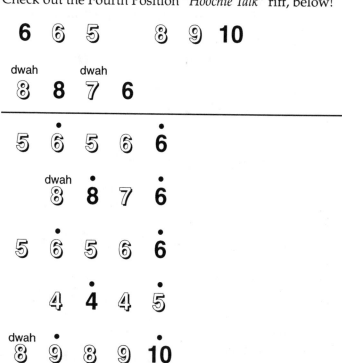

Easiest Fourth Position Blues Scales ★★

Even if you can't bend much, "dwah" the first of the two 8 out notes and you'll have a pretty good Blues Scale. Or slide (while breathing out) down the out notes to the 5 out after you hit that 8 bend, for a high/middle Blues Scale.

6 7 **8** 8b 8 9 **10**

6 7 **8** 8b slide 5 6 **6**

Other Blues Scales

The middle octave Fourth Position Blues Scale uses an overblow, and the low octave one is missing a note.

3bb 4 **4** 4### 5 6 **6** ★★★

3bb 1 **1** x 2 3 **3bb** ★★

Two Octave Blues Scale Solo ★ or ★★

Combine the high and the middle octave Fourth Position Blues Scales with some rhythm for an easy solo. Throw some good tone and wah wah on that long 6 in!

10 9 8 **8** 7 **6** 6

5 **4** 4 **4** 5 **6**••• ••• ••• •••

For a trickier version, add an extra 6 in bend (just for the heck of it), drop a note or two, throw in an unexpected 2 in, and get a mournful, biting, eight beat riff. Timing hard? Play each note for one beat, followed by 11 silent beats:

10 9 8 **8b** 8 7 **6** 6b 6

5 **4** 2 **3bb** •••

Fourth Position Minor Scales

You already know the easy one. Now try the bending versions, and then use them to play Minor melodies.

6 7 7 **8** 8 **9** 9 **10** ★

3bb 3 4 **4** 5 5 **6** 6 ★★

3bb 3 1 **1** 2 2bb **2** 3bb ★★★

Minor Melodies

You've already seen a Fourth Position Greensleeves using the higher octave Minor Scale. Now try it in the lower octave. Experiment also with *Saint James Infirmary* and *House of the Rising Sun.* You may want to play them using only half as many dots, for a bouncier or swingier feel.

A-	las	my	lo-	ve	you	do	me	wrong
3bb	4	**4**	5	**5**	5	**4**	**3**	**2**

Well	I	went	down	to
•	•	••	•	•
3bb	4	5	5	4

	Saint	James	In-	firm-	ry	••• •••
	••	•	•	•	•	
	4	5	**4**	4	**3bb**	

There	is	a	house	in	New	Or-	leans	•
•	••	•	••					
3bb	**4**	**4**	4	**3bb**	**2**	**1**	**2bb**	

They	call	the	ris-	ing	Sun	•••
•	••	•	••	•	••	
2	**3bb**	4	**3bb**	**2**	**3bb**	

Fourth Position Frankie and Johnny Blues

It's a Twelve Bar Blues with a Frankie and Johnny feel, a mix of Blues Scale and Minor Scale. Note its similarity to the verse on page 67 — the big difference is that this one really jumps around amongst the scale notes.

•		•	•		•	•	•	•••
6	7	**8**	8b	8	7	**6**	6	
I								

•		•	•		•	•	•••
6	7	**6**	6	5	**4**	5	

•	•		•		•	•	•	•••
4	**5**	6	6b	6	**5**	**4**	5	
IV								

•		•	•		•	•	•••
6	7	**8**	8b	8	7	**6**	
I							

•	•		•		•	•	••
5	6	**6**	**7**	**6**	6	5	**4**
V						IV	

•		•	•		•	•	•	••
6	7	**8**	8b	8	7	**6**	6	5 5
I								

Turnaround

Fifth Position

I'll admit it. Fifth Position is not very mainstream. It works especially well in a few important songs (like Hot Tuna's *Hesitation Blues*, with the iconoclastic Will Scarlett on harp, or Junior Well's *Quit Breakin' Down*), but you don't hear it a lot. (Although the recent movie *Mississippi Masala* used a Fifth Position harp riff as a theme song!)

Note: Some players used to reverse the terms Fifth and Fourth Positions. On page 76 I'll tell you why I don't.

It's not hard to play (you don't even need to bend, just "dwah" to sound cool), so give it a try!

Harp key is always 4 half steps below the music key.

Harp Key: C Db D Eb E F Gb G Ab A Bb B
Music Key: E F Gb G Ab A Bb B C Db D Eb

"Feel" of Position: Unusual! Offbeat! Kind of ominous, when played slowly. Best for slower Blues tunes, mostly.

Fifth Position Twelve Bar ★

Twelve Bar Octave Substitutions

Make up your own Fifth Position Octave Substitution Twelve Bar Blues by using some of these other octave notes in place of the Tonic 5 out, Subdominant 6 in, and Dominant 7 in.

Tonic (I): $2 = 5 = 8$

Subdominant (IV): $6 = 10 = 3_{bb}$

Dominant (V): $7 = 3 = 10_b$

Fancier Fifth Position Twelve Bar ★

Here's a nicer Twelve Bar to get you going on Fifth Position Blues, on the next page. This is the last Twelve Bar in which I'll use "multiple" positions: the Fifth Position Blues Scale during the Tonic parts, the Fourth Position Blues Scale during the Subdominants, and parts of the Sixth Position Blues Scale during the Dominant and Turnaround.

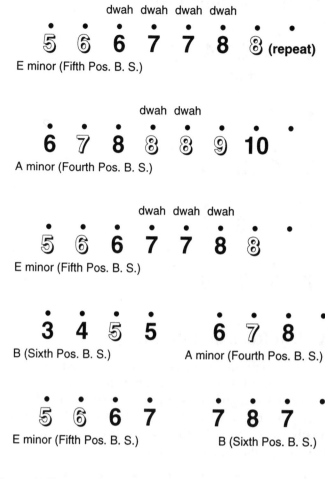

dwah dwah dwah dwah

5̇ 6̇ 6 7 7 8 8̇ (repeat)

E minor (Fifth Pos. B. S.)

dwah dwah

6 7̇ 8 8̇ 8̇ 9 10

A minor (Fourth Pos. B. S.)

dwah dwah dwah

5̇ 6̇ 6 7 7 8 8̇

E minor (Fifth Pos. B. S.)

3 4 5̇ 5   6 7̇ 8

B (Sixth Pos. B. S.)   A minor (Fourth Pos. B. S.)

5̇ 6̇ 6 7   7 8 7

E minor (Fifth Pos. B. S.)   B (Sixth Pos. B. S.)

Simplified "Blues Scales" ★

As in Fourth Position, there's no easy improv strategy for Fifth Position, other than using the Blues Scales and Easy Note Combos. Here are some no bend "Blues Scales"— The third one is similar to the *Mississippi Masala* riff.

dwah dwah

5̇ 6̇ 6 7 7 8 8̇

dwah dwah

5̇ 6̇ 6 3 3 4 5̇

5̇ 6̇ 6 7 7 slide 1 2̇

dwah

2̇ 3̇ x 3 4 5̇

Easy Note Combinations ★

These combinations of notes from the Simplified Blues Scales can always be used to create good Fifth Position riffs. Try the Fifth Position *"Hoochie Talk"* riff, on the next page!

dwah

2̇ 3̇ 3   5̇ 6̇ 6 7

dwah

7 8 8̇

Easy Note Combo Riffs

3 4 3 4 5̇

dwah
2̇ 3̇ 3̇

3 4 3 4 5̇

5̇ 6̇ 6̇ 7̇

dwah
7 8 7 8 8̇

A Neat Rock and Roll Riff

The Rolling Stones, in their hit *Miss You*, used a riff from an old British folk tune called *Lovely Joan*. The highly inventive Chicago harpist Sugar Blue chose Fifth Position to play the riff. On the recording, he adds lots of other creative and unusual Fifth Position licks — check it, and Mr. Blue's other recordings, out!

4 5 6 6 5 4 5

Fifth Position Blues Scales

2 3 3bb 3b 3 4 5 ★★

5 6 6 6### 7 8 8 ★★★

8 9 10 10bb 10b 8 8 ★★★★

Two Octave Blues Scale Riff ★

8̇ 8 7 slide to 1 2̇

Two Octave Blues Scale Solo ★★★★

2̇ 3̇ 3bb 3b 3 4 5̇

6̇ 6 6### 7 8 8̇

9 10 10bb 10b slide 1 2

Sixth Position

Sixth Position is both easy and hard for beginners. Because the Dominant note (the fifth note of the Blues Scale) can only be bent in, it's hard for beginners to play Twelve Bars in Fifth Position. But because the eerie sounding fourth note of the Blues Scale (which needs to be bent in all the commonly used positions) comes out so easily, it's great for certain riffs.

I'm indebted to Mike "Ironman" Curtis of L.A. for convincing me of the joys of Sixth Position. Ironman's an innovative harp player who's never met a position he didn't like! Catch his gigs!

Harp key is always 1 half step above the music key.

Harp Key: C Db D Eb E F Gb G Ab A Bb B
Music Key: B C Db D Eb E F Gb G Ab A Bb

"Feel" of Position: Easy to get a very downbeat and almost "grating" feel, by using lots of that "eerie" sounding 5 in — the fourth note of the Blues Scale!

Sixth Position Twelve Bar ★★

Notice that the Dominant note is a 2 in b, not the more usual 2 in bb that we use so much. You'll need to learn to hit the 2 in partly bent, instead of all the way bent — tricky! Of course, *Bending the Blues* covers it!

3	3	3	3		2	2
B					E	

3	3		2b	2		3	2b
E			Gb	E		B	Gb

Twelve Bar Octave Substitutions

Make up your own Sixth Position Octave Substitution Twelve Bar Blues by using some of these other octave notes in place of the Tonic 3 in, Subdominant 2 out, and Dominant 2 in b.

Tonic (I): **3 = 7 = 1 0b**

Subdominant (IV): **2 = 5 = 8**

Dominant (V): **2b = 5## = 9b**

Simplified "Blues Scales" ★

The missing fifth note of these scales on the next page makes it hard for beginners to hear as a Blues Scale. You might be better off concentrating on the Easy Note Combos until you can bend in the missing note.

Simplified Sixth "Blues Scales" ★

3   4   5̶   5   x   6   7

7   8   8̶   9   x   10   7

Easy Note Combinations ★

These two combinations of notes from the Simplified Blues Scales can always be used to create good Sixth Position riffs. Try the Sixth Position riff from page 57, below, with other riffs sandwiched in!

3   4   5̶   5   7   8   8̶   9

---

3   5̶·   4   3·

    3   4·   5̶   5·

3   5̶·   4   3·

    5   5̶·   4   5·

7   8̶·   8   7·

Here's another set of riffs that make a great and easy Sixth Position solo, featuring that exciting fourth note of the Blues Scale. Try the simple timing first (line one) then the real timing (line two) then swing the beat (line three).

3·   4·   5̶·   5·   5̶·   4·   3·   • • • • •

3·   4   5̶   5·   5̶   4   3·   •

3·   4   5̶   5·   5̶   4   3·   •

Finally, let's make a "solo" (longer sequence) from the riff, by repeating parts of it. Swing some or all of the beats, if you like. I'll notate it with some swing beats (third and fourth lines), but use your own sense of rhythm, too.

3·   4   5̶   5·   5̶   4   3·   •

3·   4   5̶   5·   5̶   4   3·   •

Continued on next page

Continued from previous page

˙3 4 5̲ ˙5 5̲ 4

˙3 4 5̲ ˙5 5̲ 4

˙3 4 5̲ ˙5 5̲ 4 ˙3   •

Multiple Position Blues Scale Blues

If you dare, try Fifth Position Blues Scale based riffs in the Subdominant parts, and Seventh Position riffs in the Dominant and Turnaround. I'll use the Subdom part below.

Fancier Sixth Position Twelve Bar ★

In this Twelve Bar, I'll use a rhythm variation of the great Sixth Position riff for the Tonic parts, a similar riff chosen from the Fifth Position Blues Scale notes for the first Subdominant part, and I'll fudge the rest to avoid bends!

˙3 4 5̲ ˙5 5̲ 4 ˙3 ••• (repeat)
B

5̲ 6̲ ˙6 7 6 6̲ 5̲ •••
E

˙3 4 5̲ ˙5 5̲ 4 ˙3 •••
B

•••• 5   • ••• 5̲
Gb (fudged)   E

˙3 4 5̲ ˙5 5̲ 4 ˙3 7 • • •
B   (no turnaround)

Sixth Position Blues Scales

7 8 8̲ 9 9̲b 10 7 ★★

3 1 2̲ 2bb 2b 3bb 3 ★★

3 4 5̲ 5 5̲## 6 7 ★ ★★

The Exotic Positions

The Rest of the Positions

Very few players ever use Seventh through Twelfth
Positions. I would guess that of all harmonica playing,
amateur and professional, less than one song in five or
ten thousand does. But that doesn't mean you can't!

So try some of these exotic positions, and if you like one
(or more), create your own riffs and solos in that position,
using the methods I've taught you. Why sound like
everybody else?!!!

Why is Seventh Position Called Seventh?

As I've said, I don't know where the name "positions"
originated. But I can tell you why Seventh Position is
Seventh, and Ninth is Ninth.

The Circle of Fifths

Musicians (especially jazz musicians and the more highly
trained rock musicians) use a music theory concept called
the "circle of fifths." The circle of fifths is created when
you choose any note, then choose a note that is seven half
steps above that note. Keep doing that, and you end up
on the note you started with, like this:

C - G - D - A - E - B - F#/Gb - C#/Db -

G#/Ab - D#/Eb - A#/Bb - F - C

The circle of fifths is often pictured as an actual circle, like this.

The circle of fifths has many uses, but they are beyond the
scope of this book (and covered, of course, in *Music
Theory Made Easy*). However, we find that the circle of
fifths describes the positions perfectly.

How's that? Well, if we play music in the key of "C," our
First Position harp is C, our Second Position harp is G,
our Third Position harp is D, and so on through the rest of
the circle of fifths.

I'm not sure who first came up with this. I do know that
many harp players (myself included) used to refer to
what I now call Fourth Position (key of music A, C harp)
as Fifth Position, and vice versa. But the circle of fifths
describes the positions so elegantly, that I now use what
we could call "circle of fifths position names."

Seventh Position

Harp key is always 6 half steps above the music key.

Harp Key: C Db D Eb E F Gb G Ab A Bb B
Music Key: Gb G Ab A Bb B C Db D Eb E F

Seventh Position Twelve Bar ★★★

Lots of bends in this one — make sure you only bend that 2 in down to the b, not the usual bb!

••••	••••	••••	••••		••••	••••
2b	**2**b	**2**b	**2**b		**3**	**3**
Gb					B	

••••	••••		••••	••••		••••	•••	•
2b	**2**b		**4**b	**3**		**2**b	**4**b	
Gb			Db	B		Gb	Db	

Twelve Bar Octave Substitutions

Tonic (I): $2_b = ⑤_{\#\#} = ⑨_b$

Subdominant (IV): $3 = 7 = ①⓪_b$

Dominant (V): $4_b = 1_b$

Simplified "Blues Scales"

You must be kidding! From here on in, all the Blues Scales are hard! And there are no easy note combinations — Bending Rules!

Seventh Position Blues Scales

$2_b \quad 3_{bb} \quad 3 \quad ④ \quad 4_b \quad ② \quad 2_b$ ★★

$⑨_b \quad 10 \quad ①⓪_b \quad ① \quad 1_b \quad ② \quad 2_b$ ★★

$2_b \quad 3_{bb} \quad 3 \quad ④ \quad 4_b \quad ⑤ \quad ⑤_{\#\#}$ ★ ★★

Multiple Position Blues Scale Blues

If you dare, try Sixth Position Blues Scale based riffs in the Subdominant parts, and Eighth Position riffs in the Dominant and Turnaround.

Eighth Position

Harp key is always 1 half step below the music key.

Harp Key: C Db D Eb E F Gb G Ab A Bb B

Music Key: Db D Eb E F Gb G Ab A Bb B C

Eighth Position Twelve Bar ★★★

Watch the 2 in b in the Subdominant. It's hard to make this one sound sweet!

••••	••••	••••	••••	••••	••••
1b	**1**b	**1**b	**1**b	**2**b	**2**b
Db				Gb	

••••	••••	••••	••••	•••	••• •
1b	**1**b	**3**bbb	**2**b	**1**b	**3**bbb
Db		Ab	Gb	Db	Ab

Twelve Bar Octave Substitutions

Tonic (I): $4_b = 1_b$

Subdominant (IV): $3 = 7 = 1\,0_b$

Dominant (V): $3_{bbb} = 6_b$

Eighth Position Blues Scales

1b **2** **2**b **2** **3**bbb **3** **4**b ★★★

4b **5** **5**## **6** **6**b **7** **4**b ★★★★

Something to Play With ★★★

•̇		•			•		•
5	**4**b	**3**	**4**b	**5**	**4**b	**3**	**4**b

5	**4**b	**3**	**3**bbb	**2**	**2**	**1**b	•••

5	**4**b	**3**	**4**b	**5**	**4**b	**3**	**4**b

5	**4**b	**3**	**3**bbb	**3**	**5**	**4**b	•••

Multiple Position Blues Scale Blues

If you dare, try Seventh Position Blues Scale based riffs in the Subdominant parts, and Ninth Position riffs in the Dominant and Turnaround.

Ninth Position

If you can play decent sounding Blues in Ninth Position — my hat's off to you!

Harp key is always 4 half steps above the music key.

Harp Key: C Db D Eb E F Gb G Ab A Bb B
Music Key: Ab A Bb B C Db D Eb E F Gb G

Ninth Position Twelve Bar

6b 6b 6b 6b   4b 4b
Ab   Db

6b 6b 8b 4b 6b 8b •
Ab   Eb   Db   Ab Eb

Twelve Bar Octave Substitutions

Tonic (I): 3bbb= 6b

Subdominant (IV): 4b = 1b

Dominant (V): 8b = 4###

Ninth Position Blues Scales

6b 3 4b 4 8b 9b 6b★★

3bbb 3 4b 4 4### 5## 6b ★★★★

Something to Play With ★★★

It's weird, but it works and it's something to do. And not *too* hard!

3bbb 3 • 3bbb 3 ••

3bbb slide 1 1b 3 3bbb ••

Or try fooling around with 6 in b - 7 in combos — that's about as easy as Ninth Position gets...

Multiple Position Blues Scale Blues

If you dare, try Eighth Position Blues Scale based riffs in the Subdominant parts, and Tenth Position riffs in the Dominant and Turnaround.

Tenth Position

I find this one really brutal. In my opinion, the main reason to play in Tenth Position is so you can say that you can play in Tenth Position. Sorry, but the Tonic note in this position, 8 out b or 4 out ###, is one of the least accessible notes on the ten hole harmonica!

Harp key is always 3 half steps below the music key.

Harp Key: C Db D Eb E F Gb G Ab A Bb B
Music Key: Eb E F Gb G Ab A Bb B C Db D

Tenth Position Twelve Bar

I've used two different Subdominant notes, since the 3 in bbb is easier to get to from the Dominant 3 in b. For the turnaround, try sliding down (in) from the 8 to the 3, then bending down the 3 to 3 in b.

⑧b	⑧b	⑧b	⑧b		⑥b	⑥b	
Eb					Ab		

⑧b	⑧b		③b		③bbb		⑧b	③b
Eb			Bb		Ab		Eb	Bb

Twelve Bar Octave Substitutions

Tonic (I): ⑧b = ④###

Subdominant (IV): ③bbb = ⑥b

Dominant (V): ③b = ⑥### = ①⓪bb

Easy Licks and Solos:

ha ha!

Tenth Position Blues Scales ★★★★

⑧b ⑨b ③bbb ③bb ③b ④b ④###

④### ⑤## ⑥b ⑥ ⑥### ④b ④###

Multiple Position Blues Scale Blues

If you dare, try Ninth Position Blues Scale based riffs in the Subdominant parts, and Eleventh Position riffs in the Dominant and Turnaround.

Eleventh Position

Harp key is always 2 half steps above the music key.

Harp Key: C Db D Eb E F Gb G Ab A Bb B
Music Key: Bb B C Db D Eb E F Gb G Ab A

Eleventh Position Twelve Bar

••••	••••	••••	••••		••••	••••
3b	**3**b	**3**b	**3**b		**⑧**b	**⑧**b
Bb					Eb	

••••	••••		••••		••••		••••	•••	•
3b	**3**b		**5**		**⑧**b		**3**b	**5**	
Bb			F		Eb		Bb	F	

Twelve Bar Octave Substitutions

Tonic (I): **3**b = **⑥**### = **①0**bb

Subdominant (IV): **⑧**b = **4**###

Dominant (V): **5** = **9** = **2**bb

Eleventh Position Blues Scales ★★★★

3b **4**b **4**### **⑤** **5** **6**b **⑥**###

3b **4**b **4**### **②** **2**bb **3**bbb **3**b

Something "Easy" to Do ★★

And a great exercise if you're workin' your draw bends!

•	•	••	•	•	••
6b	**5**		**6**b	**5**	

•	•	•	•	•	•	••
6b	**5**	**4**b	**3**b	**3**bbb	**3**b	

•	•	••	•	•	••
6b	**5**		**6**b	**5**	

•	•	•	•	•	•	••
6b	**5**	**4**b	**5**	**4**b	**3**b	**3**b

Multiple Position Blues Scale Blues

If you dare, try Tenth Position Blues Scale based riffs in the Subdominant parts, and Twelfth Position riffs in the Dominant and Turnaround.

Twelfth Position

Harp key is always 5 half steps below the music key.

Harp Key: C Db D Eb E F Gb G Ab A Bb B
Music Key: F Gb G Ab A Bb B C Db D Eb E

Twelfth Position Twelve Bar

•••• •••• •••• ••••   •••• ••••
2bb 2bb 2bb 2bb   **3b 3b**
F   Bb

•••• ••••   ••••   ••••   •••• •••
2bb 2bb   4̶   **3b**   **2bb** 4̶   •
F   C   Bb   F   C

Twelve Bar Octave Substitutions

Tonic (I): **5 = 9 = 2bb**

Subdominant (IV): **3b =** 6̶### = 1̶ 0̶bb

Dominant (V): 1̶ = 4̶ = 7̶ = 1̶0̶

Twelfth Position Blues Scales ★★★★

5 **6b** 6̶### **7** 7̶ 8̶b **9**

2bb 3bbb 3b 3 4̶ 4̶### **5**

Something Easy to Do

5 6b 7̶ 7̶   •   **5 6b** 7̶ 7̶   •

5 6b 7̶ 7̶ **6b 5**   •••

An Offbeat Major Scale ★★

Why use Twelfth Position to play a Major Scale? Because it's there, and not *too* hard.

2bb 2 3bb 3b 4̶ **4** 5̶ **5**

Multiple Position Blues Scale Blues

If you dare, try Eleventh Position Blues Scale based riffs in the Subdominant parts, and First Position riffs in the Dominant and Turnaround.

PART THREE

Playing By Yourself

When you're playing harmonica all by yourself, using the positions are easy. There's really only **one question** you need to ask yourself, and that's which position you're going to choose to play in.

So grab any key harmonica that you like — it doesn't matter now. Choose the position — any position — that you want to work on, and study my suggestions for that position. Then play scales, riffs, and solos at whatever level of technical expertise that you can manage.

It's important to do this — musicians call it **"woodshedding."** That means working on your playing by yourself, as though you were out in the woodshed. Playing by yourself is a great way of getting to know the positions — how they feel (more sad? happy? Bluesy?), what licks you like, which scales you can manage (and which you can't, at least not in public).

But after you feel comfortable with a few (or more) of the positions, you may want to play along with other musicians. And that brings up a whole new issue — which key harmonica to use when.

Playing With Other Musicians

As soon as you decide to play your harmonica with other musicians, new questions come up — questions which you must be able to answer if you want to play with others, with confidence.

One question, though, I am not going to cover much. And that's "What Style of Music Are We Going to Play?"

For the purposes of this book, I assume that you are going to be playing Blues music, or styles of Rock music that are based on the Blues. Lots of other styles of harmonica playing exist, and I've covered them in other books. With Blues or Blues-based rock in mind, let's keep going.

Which Positions Can I Play?

If you've done some woodshedding on positions, you'll be able to answer this one. For example, I'd be glad to go out and jamm with anyone right now, using positions One to Six. But I'd have to spend a good few minutes reviewing scales for any of the others — Seventh through Twelfth — before I got on stage with the intent to use them!

For starters, practice playing in First, Second, and Third Positions by yourself, and memorize the three Simplest Position Rules (they're great to fall back on) plus at least one easy Twelve Bar Blues for each.

Who's In Charge of Key?

Before you start to play with others, you need to know the answer to this question. Of course, playin' with an old friend on the front porch is different than stepping up on stage to sit in with a band that you've never met before.

In the first situation, "What key shall we play in?" can be a negotiated discussion between the players. The key might even depend on what key harp you like best, and what position.

In the second, you may well be expected to play in the key chosen by the band. The bandleader will say: "Blues in the key of A." If you don't have a harp in a key that you can use in a position you know that comes out in the key of A — well, in the words of an old Blues friend: "When in doubt, lay out!"

Dealin' with the Band

Of course, sometimes a band will ask the invited harp player what key he or she wants to play. If they do, be ready with a clear, reasonable, answer. What's reasonable? Well, although good bands can play in any key, most bands like songs in E, A, G, C, or D the best. Any other keys may be trickier for them — so make it easy, and choose a position and harmonica that uses one of these five popular music keys.

NOTE: Other musicians sometimes assume that harp players don't know which harp to use, and will try to tell you "Use your A harp." Aside from being rude and condescending, this does not give *you* the choice of what position to use. If this happens, the proper response is: "What key is the song in?" Then you can make up your own mind about what key harmonica, and what position, to use. If they resist, see "Talking the Talk," below, for a good response.

Ready to Blow the Blues!

Before you begin to play with other musicians using positions, you should feel comfortable about the following things. This is especially important if you are planning to play with people who are not already friends.

• You've started to get a sense of the different "feels" of the different positions.

• You understand the Twelve Bar Blues, including "Intros."

• You know which positions you can play, and which ones are not yet ready for prime time.

• You know who gets to choose the key (you or the other players).

When You Pick the Key

If the key choice is **yours,** the style of music (slow or fast, sad or upbeat) is probably yours too.

• Start out by explaining that you want to play a Twelve Bar Blues (or a Twelve Bar Rock Blues).

• Choose your harmonica key and position. Make sure it produces a "reasonable" key choice for the band, like E, A, G, C, or D.

• Decide on using an intro or not. If you want an intro, decide whether to use a two bar or four bar form.

• Tell the others what you're going to do, and either count off "one two three four" or ask someone else to do the count. You're on!

This can be done quickly. Just say something like: "Let's do a Twelve Bar Blues in the key of E, with a two bar intro. Mournful, Minor feeling, and slow, like this — One Two Three Four." You've got your D harp in hand to play some slow, sad, Third Position Blues in E, and you're on!

When They Pick the Key

If the key choice is going to be **theirs,** you'll need the answers to at least one, and preferably four, questions.

• Most important, "What key is the song in?"

• "Slow, fast or medium?" Listening to the count of "one two three four" will let you know the speed of the song before you begin to play. But it won't give you enough time to choose a position based on the speed of the music.

• "Sad or happy?" More advance info that will help you to choose your position. You could also ask something like "Happy feel or more Minor?"

•"Starting on an intro or the Twelve Bar?" is also helpful to know, but you can always wait and hear what's going on with the intro if you don't want to ask too many questions.

If the situation does not seem to be one in which lots of questions will be appreciated, just find out the key of the song, and start out in Second Position. Wait until you can hear the tempo (speed) and whether there is an intro or not before you start to play.

IMPORTANT: If you're not used to playing with others: Don't play too loudly, and don't play when anyone else is singing or doing a solo. It's much better to be asked to play more and louder than to be asked to shut up!

My Position Strategy

If I'm not absolutely sure what a song is going to be like, I usually start out with the correct key Second Position harmonica in my mouth, and the correct key First and Third position harmonicas in easy reach, just in case it turns out that the song would be better in First or Third.

The PositionFinder™ Method

You've done your homework and your woodshedding. You've at the jamm session, on stage, and asked the questions and gotten your answers. Now how do you remember which key harp to use with which key music?

You have three choices. You can either memorize the Harp Key/Music Key charts, starting with First, Second, and Third Positions, then adding the others that you choose to use.

You can memorize the "Counting Half Step" method (page 51), and learn to do it FAST.

Or you can make a **PositionFinder™** and spend a minute learning to use it.

The PositionFinder™ is based on a similar invention of mine, The NoteFinder™. The NoteFinder™, included in each copy of my book *Music Theory Made Easy*, is a simple device that automatically tells you the letter names of the notes of any kind of scale (Blues, Major, Minor, and Pentatonic) in any key. It also tells you what notes make up all the most important types of chords in any key.

The PositionFinder™ tells you what key harmonica to use with which key music. Follow the directions on this page and the next, and make your own PositionFinder™!

The Outer Circle

There are twelve letter names arranged around the outside of the outer circle, below. These can represent either a Music Key or a Harmonica Key. I have given you both the sharp # and the flat b names for notes that have both. Get used to the note arrangement — all the #/b notes are on one side — you'll need to find notes, quickly.

(Don't have easy access to a copy machine? You can trace this circle and the letters if you need to.)

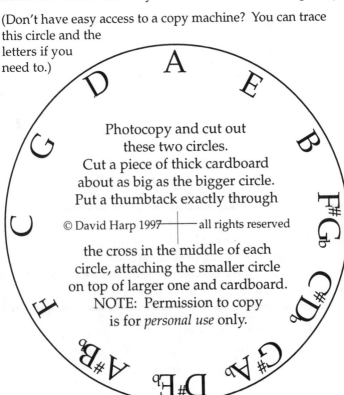

Photocopy and cut out
these two circles.
Cut a piece of thick cardboard
about as big as the bigger circle.
Put a thumbtack exactly through

the cross in the middle of each
circle, attaching the smaller circle
on top of larger one and cardboard.
NOTE: Permission to copy
is for *personal use* only.

The Inner Circle

There are markings arranged around the outside of the inner circle. The **M marks M2 - M6** will line up with the letter names on the outer circle to show you **Music Keys.** The **H marks H2 - H6** will line up with the letter names on the outer circle to show you **Harmonica keys.**

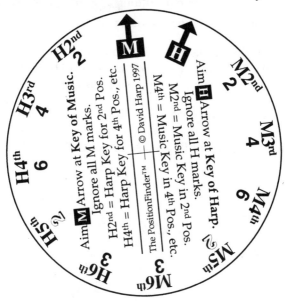

The Finished PositionFinder™

This is what a finished PositionFinder™ should look like. Note thumbtack in center.

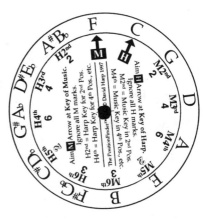

Two Ways to Use Your PositionFinder™

The PositionFinder™ works in two ways:

• If you know the **Music Key** that you are going to be playing in, the PositionFinder™ will tell you what the correct key harmonica is for each position.

• If you know **what key Harmonica** you are going to use, the PositionFinder™ will tell you what the correct music keys are for each position on that harmonica.

If you can remember that "M" means "Music Key," and that "H" means "Harmonica Key", and if you can count to six — it's easy!

IMPORTANT: You must always decide whether:

• You already know the **key of the music**, and want the correct harmonica keys for the different positions...

• Or you already know **which key harmonica** you want to use and are looking for the correct music keys for the different positions.

If You Know the <u>Key of the Music</u>

Your guitarist pal yells out "Let's play a Blues in B!"
What harp (or harps) do you grab? It's really easy!

- Locate the letter name B on the **outer** circle.

- Turn the **inner** circle until the **M** (for **M**usic Key)
arrow points at the B on the outer circle.

- Look at the marks **H2ⁿᵈ - H6ᵗʰ** on the **inner** circle.
Ignore the M marks! Each **"H" mark (for Harmonica
key)** lines up with a letter name on the outer circle.

- The letter name next to H2ⁿᵈ tells you **what key
<u>Harp</u> to use for Second Position, when you're playing
a Blues in the key of B. And so on for H3ʳᵈ to H6ᵗʰ!

Hint: Hold it
so that H marks
are on the top
side, and easy
to see!

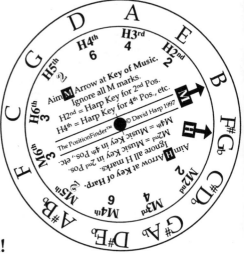

Check
These Out
on the Diagram!

<u>H2ⁿᵈ</u> will be lined up near the note name E on the outer
circle. If you play a Blues in B, the correct **Second Position Harmonica** to use will be an "E" harp.

<u>H3ʳᵈ</u> will be lined up near the note name A on the outer
circle. If you play a Blues in B, the correct **Third Position
Harmonica** to use will be an "A" harp.

<u>H4ᵗʰ</u> will be lined up near the note name D. If you play a
Blues in B, the correct **Fourth Position Harmonica** to use
will be an "D" harp.

<u>H5ᵗʰ</u> will be lined up near the note name G. If you play a
Blues in B, the correct **Fifth Position Harmonica** to use
will be an "G" harp.

<u>H6ᵗʰ</u> will be lined up near the note name C. If you play a
Blues in B, the correct **Sixth Position Harmonica** to use
will be a "C" harp.

You now have six choices of harmonica to use. Depending on whether you know the "feel" of the song that's
coming, or what harps you have, you can make a choice.
Or choose a few harps, and have 'em ready for action!

Helpful Tab Hint

For your convenience, I've put the HarpTab™ for the
most important note of each position (like 2 in for Second
Position, 4 in for Third, and so on) directly under the "H"
and "M" marks for each position on the inner circle.

If You've Chosen <u>What Key Harp</u> to Use

Your favorite harmonica today is your Eb (E flat). Your playin' partners ask you what key you'd like to play in. You're in a Fifth Position mood. What key do you use?

- Locate the letter name D#/Eb on the **outer** circle (Remember that D# = Eb? If not, review page 9).

- Turn the **inner** circle until the 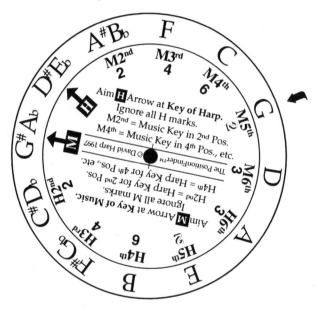 arrow **(for <u>H</u>arp key)** points at the D#/Eb on the outer circle.

- Look at the **M2ⁿᵈ - M6ᵗʰ** marks on the **inner** circle. Ignore the H marks! See how each **"M"** mark lines up with a letter name on the outer circle.

- The letter name next to M 5ᵗʰ tells you **what key the <u>M</u>usic is in when you play** in Fifth Position on your key of Eb harp. You call out "Blues in G!"

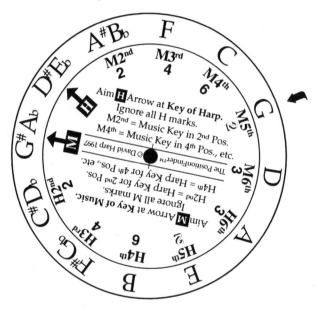

Check These Out on the Diagram

M2ⁿᵈ will be lined up near the note name Bb on the outer circle. If you're using a key of Eb harp, the **Music Key** produced by playing **Second Position** will be Bb.

M3ʳᵈ will be lined up near the note name F on the outer circle. If you are using a key of Eb harmonica, the **Music Key** produced by playing **Third Position** will be F.

M4ᵗʰ will be lined up near the note name C on the outer circle. If you are using a key of Eb harp, the **Music Key** produced by playing **Fourth Position** will be C.

M5ᵗʰ will be lined up near the note name G on the outer circle. If you are using a key of Eb harmonica, the **Music Key** produced by playing **Fifth Position** will be G.

M6ᵗʰ will be lined up near the note name D on the outer circle. If you are using a key of Eb harmonica, the **Music Key** produced by playing **Sixth Position** will be D.

You can now easily decide which of the six positions to use (depending on your mood and the "feel" of the song you want to play). Just choose a position, shout out the correct music key to your partners, and let 'er rip!

More Charts

In addition to the PositionFinder™, here are some charts that you may find useful. Copy* them, and paste or tape them onto either your carrying case or onto individual harmonica boxes (depending on which type of chart it is).
* Permission to copy these charts is for personal use only.

Individual Harp Position Charts

These charts are for putting on **each individual harp case**, and tell you what **music keys** you can play with **that harp.**

1	2	3	4	5	6	
C	**G**	**D**m	**A**m	**E**	**B**	© D. Harp 1997 All rights reserved
4	2	4	6	②	3	

- Stick the one just above onto your key of C harp case.

- The **top row** of numbers refer to **Positions, 1 to 6.**

- The **middle row** of letter names tell you **which key music** you will be playing in that position on that harmonica. So on your key of C harp, in Fifth Position you will be playing music in the key of E.

- The little **"m" symbols** remind you that Third and Fourth Position are often used in **sad or Minor** Blues.

- The **bottom row** has HarpTab™ to remind you of the **most important note** for that position.

Here are the other key charts. The letter name under the 1 is the harp key, since in First Position the key of harp and music are the same. **MEMORIZE these #/b names — your partners may use a # name to tell you the key!**

C#=Db D#=Eb F#=Gb G#=Ab A#=Bb

1	2	3	4	5	6	
Db	**Ab**	**Eb**m	**Bb**m	**F**	**C**	© D. Harp 1997 All rights reserved
4	2	4	6	②	3	

1	2	3	4	5	6	
D	**A**	**E**m	**B**m	**Gb**	**Db**	© D. Harp 1997 All rights reserved
4	2	4	6	②	3	

1	2	3	4	5	6	
Eb	**Bb**	**F**m	**C**m	**G**	**D**	© D. Harp 1997 All rights reserved
4	2	4	6	②	3	

1	2	3	4	5	6	
E	**B**	**Gb**m	**Db**m	**Ab**	**Eb**	© D. Harp 1997 All rights reserved
4	2	4	6	②	3	

1	2	3	4	5	6
F	C	Gm	Dm	A	E
4	2	4	6	2	3

1	2	3	4	5	6
Gb	Db	Abm	Ebm	Bb	F
4	2	4	6	2	3

1	2	3	4	5	6
G	D	Am	Em	B	Gb
4	2	4	6	2	3

1	2	3	4	5	6
Ab	Eb	Bbm	Fm	C	G
4	2	4	6	2	3

1	2	3	4	5	6
A	E	Bm	Gbm	Db	Ab
4	2	4	6	2	3

1	2	3	4	5	6
Bb	F	Cm	Gm	D	A
4	2	4	6	2	3

1	2	3	4	5	6
B	Gb	Dbm	Abm	Eb	Bb
4	2	4	6	2	3

The above individual harp key charts are good when you know which key harp you want to use, and need to know what key music is played in each position on that harp.

Three Position Chart for All Music Keys

This next harp case chart will help if you know the **key of the music first.** It tells you what key harmonicas to use in the three most popular positions — First, Second, and Third — when you *already know the music key.*

The band leader calls out the key of the song: "Bb Blues!"

• Find the **music key** — Bb — in the **top row.** That's the *column* you'll be looking in.

• The correct First Position harp key will be the same as the music key, in the **top row.** Then look down:

• The **correct Second Position harp key** will be in the middle row **of that column:** Eb.

• The **correct** Third Position harp key will be the **bottom row of that column:** Ab.

G	Ab	A	Bb	B	C	Db	D	Eb	E	F	Gb
C	Db	D	Eb	E	F	Gb	G	Ab	A	Bb	B
F	Gb	G	Ab	A	Bb	B	C	Db	D	Eb	E

One Last Chart — More Music Keys

Here's one last chart that many of my more serious students like to study in their spare time. It basically gives you the same music key information as The PositionFinder™ does, but in a chart format.

> • The leftmost column — marked "Music & First" — gives you the music key (and the First Position Harp key, which is always the same as the music key).
>
> • The rest of the columns — marked "Second Pos. H." through "Sixth Pos. H." tell you the right key of harmonica to use for the music key in the leftmost column.

I've given you both sharp and flat names here. Some players like to get an enlarged copy of this, and put it on their harp carry case.

Music & First	Second Pos. H.	Third Pos. H.	Fourth Pos. H.	Fifth Pos. H.	Sixth Pos. H.
C	F	A# Bb	D# Eb	G# Ab	C# Db
C# Db	F# Gb	B	E	A	D
D	G	C	F	A# Bb	D# Eb
D# Eb	G# Ab	C# Db	F# Gb	B	E
E	A	D	G	C	F
F	A# Bb	D# Eb	G# Ab	C# Db	F# Gb
F# Gb	B	E	A	D	G
G	C	F	A# Bb	D# Eb	G# Ab
G# Ab	C# Db	F# Gb	B	E	A
A	D	G	C	F	A# Bb
A# Bb	D# Eb	G# Ab	C# Db	F# Gb	B
B	E	A	D	G	C
C	F	A# Bb	D# Eb	G# Ab	C# Db

Talking the Talk

If you've learned what's in this book, and want your playing partners to know that you know a bit of music theory, read the following statements. Then put them into your own words when you discuss what harp to use.

"For lots of Blues, I use the "Cross Harp" or Myxolydian ("Mix-oh-**lid**-ee-an") based Blues Scale in Second Position. That's pretty versatile, for any type of Blues.

"But if it's a Minor key Blues, I sometimes use a Dorian-Minor based Blues Scale in Third Position, or an Aeolian ("A- **oh**- lee-an") Minor based Blues Scale in Fourth Position. They let me throw in some Minor Scale notes."

"And if it's a really upbeat, bouncy, Major feeling Blues, I might use First Position, since then it's easy to add lots of Major Scale notes in with the Blues Scale."

Of course, make sure that you can use these positions — you may have to put your harp where your mouth is!

Sales Pitch

I know that it may sound, to some of you, that I've been relentlessly plugging other books throughout this one.

Sorry about that, but there's so much to learn about harmonica that if I put everything in one book, it would be a thousand pages long, and only the largest universities could afford to buy it!

And certain things — like Bending and Music Theory — are so important and useful to harp players that it's hard not to mention them...

So if you've found this book to be useful, I'm going to assume that you might be interested in hearing about some of my other book, tapes, and video products. I'll start out by telling you about some products that can be used by beginners or advanced beginners, as well as some products that can help anyone be a better musician!

Three Minutes to™ Blues Harmonica!

This 73 minute video is my easiest Blues method yet! Using my incredible Harmonica Hand Signals™, I'll have you blowing your first Blues in just three minutes! So if you can't already improvise simple Second Position Blues or play Twelve Bars, get this one. After an hour or so with the video you'll appreciate and be ready to use positions (and *this* book) much more easily! And if you can already play Blues, give this one to a friend, and create your own jamming partner! Three Minutes to Blues Harmonica video, 73 minutes: **$12.95**. With "C" harmonica, just **$17.95** for a lifetime of the Blues!

Instant Blues Harmonica

This is my "classic," if you prefer your information in book and audiotape form — over 150,000 satisfied users! It covers everything you need to know to play simple Blues in First, Second, and Third Positions, even if you've never blown a note before. 64 page book and 90 minute playalong tape (for key of "C" harp) just **$12.95**.

C & W Harmonica Made Easy

If you like the sound of C & W, here's an entire book devoted to creating songs, solos, and riffs using the super easy but satisfying "Country Pentatonic" Scale described on page 39. For beginners or pros! 64 page book $4.95, with 90 minute tape (for "C" harp) only $12.95.

Music Theory Made Easy

If you really want to understand music theory (as well as harmonica theory) — this one's for you! All the scales and chord structures you need to know if you want to improvise many kinds of music (including Blues, rock, country, pop, and even some jazz) or compose your own songs — without needing to read music!

You'll also learn why the scales are the way they are, how to really use Roman Numeral names and the circle of fifths, and much more. The 80 page book is **only $5.95.** With the 90 minute tape (including lots of examples demonstrated on harmonica), **$12.95.**

The Pocket Harmonica Songbook

This easy to use book features over 40 of the world's best loved songs — folk, Blues, spirituals, holiday songs, even some classical! Many of the songs are so simple you'll play them instantly!

Lots of songs included that were mentioned (as examples) in this book, like: *St. James Infirmary* (4th Pos.), *St. Louis Blues* (1st Pos.), *Good Mornin' Blues* (2nd and 3rd Pos.), three different *Boogie Woogies*, *Frankie and Johnnie* (1st and 2nd Pos.), and *Oh When The Saints* (2nd Pos.). Plus *This Train, Scarborough Fair, Bach's Chorale, Down in the Valley,* and many other of your country and folk favorites! 64 page book only $4.95, for use with any key harmonica.

Bending the Blues

Add 16 new "bent notes" to your regular ten hole harmonica — and be able to play *all* the "Two Star" and "Three Star" songs in *this* book! (The "Four Star" riffs I can't guarantee!) This 64 page book and 90 minute cassette covers *everything* you'll ever need to know about bending. From getting that first feeble bend, to using easy 2, 4, 5, and 6 in bends. From breaking the 3 hole in into four useable notes, to overblowing 4, 5, and 6 out!

Full of scales and licks! Use with A, C, and F ten hole harps. The American Harmonica Newsletter reviewed this one and called it: "...THE most important book and cassette on Blues harp!" Book **$4.95,** book & cassette **only $12.95. It will help you instantly, plus give you years of good stuff to work on, no matter what your level!**

Coming Soon: *Books on Improvisation with Riffs,* and *High Harp!*

Play Like (And WITH) The Pros! *Juke* & the Blues Masters Harmonica Tape/CD!

You've got to listen to the pros if you really want to learn the Blues! Here's a two part program to help you!

The Blues Masters Harmonica CD ($17.95) has 18 of the best harp songs ever, played by the original artists (14 songs are on the tape, **$9.95**) including Little Walter, Big Walter, Charlie Musselwhite, and many more. Buy it and you'll get a **FREE** two page **hint sheet,** which describes the key, position, and an improvising strategy for playing along with each song! With a "C" and an "A" harp you can play many of the songs, add a "Bb" harp and play most of them!

My new *"Juke"* cassette is 90 minutes long, and describes in easy to play detail every note, lick, and bend of Little Walter's immortal song *Juke* (original* on both CD and tape). Easiest way ever to learn from a master! For **key of "A" harp, $8.95.** (* Recorded 5/12/52, Arc Music Corp., BMI).

Instant Blues Harmonica Volume Two

This sequel to "IBH" Volume One on page 93 is for advanced beginner and intermediate players. Although not my most beautiful looking book, it has lots of great info on bending, tone, throat vibrato, First, Second, and Third Positions, and loads of great riffs and solos in a variety of Blues and Rock styles. 32 page book and 90 minute tape (for "A" harp) **$12.95.**

Instant Chromatic Harmonica: The Blues/Jazz Improvisation Method

It's actually easier for beginners to play great sounding Blues in the style of Little Walter on "chro" than on the ten hole. The holes are bigger, good tone comes easier, and bending isn't necessary! And if you can already play songs on chro but can't improvise, this will help — fast!

This 112 page book and 90 minute tape starts off with Little Walter Blues style, then goes on to the more complex styles of Stevie Wonder and Toots Thielemans. If you've always been scared to try chro, *you owe it to yourself* to try this method for an hour or so! And we'll give you a good deal on a chromatic harp! Book & cassette only **$19.95.**

Instant Harmonica for Kids!

Give the lifelong gift of music — and fun! A great music education for ages 4 - 9, combining my decades of experience with techniques from Suzuki, Orff-Schulwerk, and other children's methods. 64 page book, 90 min. tape, "C" harp $14.95, Book/tape **$9.95! Teachers: call for a deal!**

The Instant Video Kit for Kids! A great introduction to folk, Blues, rock, and classical harmonica for kids ages five to ten! See David as a rock star, or as Beethoven! **$14.95 with C harmonica, $9.95 without!** 33 minutes VHS.

Guitar! Flute! Harmonicas!

Instant Flute — 64 page book and high quality "fipple" flute, great for Blues or folk songs, only $14.95.

Instant Guitar — an 80 page book, 90 minute cassette and "ChordSnaffle™" — which lets you play chords using only one finger! Play super simple Blues, rock, folk, classical, country, or even jazz songs within minutes (for beginners only), $12.95. Who needs jamming partners when you can play all by yourself?!!!

Harps hard to find? Give us a call!

For Teachers & Wholesale Accounts

Want to teach adults or children? We'd love to help! We'll provide you with books, tapes, and harps at a volume discount you can't refuse. Use them as fund-raisers for schools or community groups! Also, call us for great wholesale volume discounts! Our beginning packages sell in book, toy, gift, hospital, and outdoor stores and catalogs!

Personal Appearances

I do unique workshops and seminars integrating har-monica and psychology for corporations or groups of *any* kind — please write for brochure!

---

musical i press

P.O. Box 1561-PO, Montpelier, Vermont 05602
Phone Orders call (802) 223-1544   (Fax: 223-0543)
Have Visa, MC, AmEx Card and know just what you want? Call our Automated order line:
1 (800) MOJO - IS - I   (665 - 6474)

To Order: Call in your order or send a check or money order. Please clearly identify the items you want, and include the following shipping charges. We ship via UPS unless otherwise instructed.

U.S. Orders: Please add $4 for the first item, plus $1 for each additional item.

Canadian Orders: Please add $6 for the first item, $2 for each additional item.

Other Foreign Orders: We'll charge your Visa or MasterCard or American Express Card exactly what it costs us to ship, or else call/fax/write for charges.